The Ritual Gem of
the Oriental and Eastern Churches

THE DIVINE LITURGY

The Mystery of the Kingdom

BOOK 3

THE CREED TO THE INSTITUTION NARRATIVE

By

Father Athanasius al-Makary

Nuns of St. Mary & St. Demiana Convent
Georgia, USA

Translator

Mena Fawzy Abdelsayed

Editor-in-Chief

THE DIVINE LITURGY
The Mystery of the Kingdom
BOOK 3

THE CREED TO THE INSTITUTION NARRATIVE

The Ritual Gem of the Coptic Church Between the Oriental and Eastern Churches

By Father Athanasius al-Makary

Copyright © 2022 by Mena Fawzy Abdelsayed

All rights reserved.

No part of this publication may be reproduced, stored in a retrieval system, or transmitted in any form or by any means — electronic, mechanical, graphic, photocopy, recording, taping, information storage, or any other — without written permission of the copyright owner.

Published by:
St. Mary & St. Moses Abbey Press
101 S Vista Dr., Sandia, TX 78383
stmabbeypress.com

INTRODUCTION TO THE RITUALS OF THE COPTIC CHURCH

This publication was originally available in Arabic in a series of books called *Al-Durra al-Taqsiyya Li-l-Kanīsa al-Qibṭiyya* (The Ritual Gem of the Coptic Church). It outlines the spiritual and deep rituals of the sacraments, feasts and fasts of the Coptic Church in light of the other Oriental and Eastern Churches. This detailed work is found in fifty books in Arabic and focuses on the historical developments of the liturgical life of the Church from the first century onwards based on the writings of the Church Fathers, and the manuscripts and the national and international academic studies of the Coptic liturgy.

TABLE OF CONTENTS

THE ORTHODOX CREED AND HAND WASHING 9

THE RECONCILIATION PRAYER AND THE KISS OF PEACE 40

PRO-ANAPHORAL SECTION: THE GREATER THANKSGIVING PRAYER 81

CHERUBIC PRAISE..122

HOLY, HOLY, HOLY..136

THE INSTITUTION 156

Bibliography..*194*

ABBREVIATIONS

ANF	*Ante-Nicene Fathers*
BnF	*Bibliothèque nationale de France*
NPNF	*Nicene and Post-Nicene Fathers*
OCP	*Orientalia Christiana Periodica*
ODCC	*The Oxford Dictionary of the Christian Church*
PG	*Patrologia Graeca*

THE ORTHODOX CREED AND HAND WASHING

First: The Orthodox Creed (Canon)

Introduction

Creed, from the Greek origin κανών (canon) means *"straight rod."* It also means *rule* or *standard*.[1] For Paul the Apostle, it points to the *sphere* of apostolic work,[2] or, practical *rules* in the Christian life.[3] For the Syrians, it means *order*.

Canon has other synonyms. For Syrians, *canons* are known as *Sonon* (methods). They are termed *Shara'e* (law) in Arabic. As for the word, *Destoūr* (code or constitution), it is Persian, not Arabic.

Clement of Rome mentioned *canon* in his Epistle to the Corinthians (passage 7) towards the end of the first century, referring to *the glorious and venerable rule*[4] and the baptismal creed, which Irenaeus of Lyons (130-200 AD) labels as *the canon of truth*.[5] The Council of Antioch (269 AD) also referred to *the canon*.[6] Clement of

---

[1] See *American Heritage Dictionary* under *Canon*.
[2] 2 Corinthians 10.13,15
[3] Galatians 6.16
[4] *ANF01*, 1886, 10.7.
[5] *Ibid.*, 471 (Against Heresies, 1.9.4). Translated as *the rule of the truth*.
[6] *NPNF2-14*, 1899, 158 (Canon I of the Council of Antioch): translated as *the decree*.

Alexandria (150-215 AD) spoke of the *canon of truth*.[7] Eusebius of Caesarea (260-340) pointed to *the canon of the truth*,[8] and, *the canon of the preaching*.[9] He also referred to *the ecclesiastical canon*[10] which recognized no other Gospels than the four. Basil of Caeserea (330-379 AD) wrote of *the transmitted canon of true religion*.[11] The First Ecumenical Council of Nicaea (325 AD) does not apply the term to its own enactments, yet the Second Ecumenical Council of Constantinople (381 AD) did use *canons*[12] to label this work. Athanasius of Alexandria (328-373) used *canon* to refer in a broad sense to *ecclesiastical canons*.[13] At first, *canon* applied to all clergy; hence, any cleric might be called κανονικός. The first canon of the Council of Antioch (convening in 341) admitted *the holy canon* in reference to *the rule of the clerical life*. *Canon* applied to *canonical singers* in the Council of Laodicea (341-381).[14]

In the Byzantine and the Syrian churches, the word *canon* is a traditional term referring to their order of liturgical praises.

---

[7] *ANF02*, 275 (*Exhortation to Heathens*, Chapter 10): translated as *law of truth*.
[8] Eusebius of Caesarea, *Ecclesiastical History*, 4.23.
[9] *Ibid*., 238 (Eusebius of Caesarea, *Ecclesiastical History*, 3.32). Translated as *the sound norm of the preaching*.
[10] *Ibid*., 434; (Eusebius of Caesarea, *Ecclesiastical History*, 6.25).
[11] Letter 204. Translated there as *the rule of godliness delivered*.
[12] Socrates, *Ecclesiastical History*, 1.13.
[13] Encyclical Letters 1&2.
[14] *NPNF2-14*, 40-41.

Although *canon* applies to any Church service, it refers specifically to the main invariable body of prayer during the Divine Liturgy, also known as the *Anaphora*.[15]

Canon also refers to *"a table for the calculation of Easter."*[16]

Canons of Faith and their Various Articulations

The *Creed of Faith* (Τὸ σύμβολον) is a shortened formula of the primary tenets of Christian doctrine. The traditional example of this is the *Nicene Creed* of faith in the East. In the Christian West, it is the *Apostles' Creed*.

The *Creed of faith* is essentially the abbreviated faith formula memorized by the catechumens, recited before their immersion into the baptismal water.[17] The details of this creed varied from place to another.

What is certain is that before the middle of the second century, the confession of the catechumen was developed to a form accepted by all the major churches. Writings concerning the contents of this confession may be found in the writings of Irenaeus of Lyons (130-200 AD), Tertullian of Carthage (160-225 AD),[18] Novatian,[19] Origen of Alexandria (180-254 AD),[20] and others. They

---

[15] *NPNF2-14*, 41.
[16] *Ibid*.
[17] Dix, Gregory. *The Shape of The Liturgy*, (London: Dacre Press, 1945), 486.
[18] *ANF03*, 980.
[19] *On the Trinity*, I-VIII.
[20] Smith, William, and Samuel Cheetham. *Dictionary of Christian Antiquities*. Vol. 1, (London: William Clowes and Sons, 1876), 489.

all agree on the essence of this confirmation, with slight variations in expression.

After the middle of the second century, this confession took on a new form, due to the gnostic debates, and thus became an official canon, taking on the label of *Canon of Truth* or *Canon of Faith*. Thus, it became a criterion for exposing the fallacies of the heretics.[21]

With the arrival of the fourth century, these various formulae specific to baptism began to revolve around the concept of the Trinity in agreement with the writing of Matthew the Evangelist.[22] The *Creed of Faith* then became the confession recited at baptism in all places, East and West.[23]

In the final stages of their catechism and before receiving holy baptism, the catechumens memorized the *Creed of Faith* to recite it from memory before the bishop or priest, as an official confession of the Christian faith. Then, this creed was used in the era of dogmatic disagreements, as a framework to determine the foundations of the upright faith, protecting the church from heretics and heresies.

In this regard, Canon 46 of the local Council of Laodicea (341-381) states:

---

[21] Dix, *op. cit.*, 485-486.
[22] Matthew 28.19
[23] Smith and Cheetham, *op. cit.*, 489.

> They who are to be baptized must learn the faith [Creed] by heart, and recite it to the bishop, or to the presbyters, on the fifth day of the week.[24]

The *week* is that of the Passover or the Holy Passion Week. The *fifth day* is Covenant Thursday. The first rituals of Holy baptism, which is renouncing of Satan, began the next day on Good Friday. The Baptism took place on the eve of the Resurrection Feast.

The First Ecumenical Council of Nicaea (325 AD) followed by the Ecumenical Council of Constantinople (381 AD) placed the *Creed of Faith* that we know today. It became the statement of the one faith in the Orthodox Church, and it quickly spread thereafter.

The Coptic Church, until today, continues to use in the baptism rite a very ancient form of the creed, one that predates the Nicene-Constantinople Creed.

Apostles' Creed

The *Apostolic Canon* or *Apostles' Creed* is a formula of faith used only in the Christian West.[25] It was used since 390 AD by Ambrose of Milan (339-397 AD),[26] and is considered among the oldest creeds of faith, attributed to the twelve apostles. It is an abbreviated version of the Nicene Creed known to the Christian East, yet it contains subtle differences.

---

[24] *NPNF2-14*, 221. This is the same as Canon 78 of the local Council of Trullo in 692.
[25] Bible encyc. Vol 4, 107.
[26] *NPNF2-10*, 618 (Epistle 20.4).

Apostolic Canon or *Apostles' Creed* has two different versions, one short and another long. The shorter version, known as the *Old Roman* or *Latin Creed*, dates to the mid-second century (about 140 AD). This formula was transmitted to us through Marcellus of Ancyra in 341 AD. The longer version in its current form stems from a much later date. It took its final shape in southern Gaul (France), but most probably not before the mid-fifth century (perhaps one or two segments come from the seventh century). What follows is the text:

1) The Old Roman (Latin) Text

> I believe in God the Father Almighty, and in Jesus Christ, His only Son, our Lord; who was by the Holy Ghost born of the Virgin Mary; under Pontius Pilate, was crucified, and buried; the third day he rose from the dead; He ascended into heaven, and sitteth on the right hand of the Father; from thence he shall come to judge the quick and the dead. And in the Holy Ghost; the holy Church; the forgiveness of sins; the resurrection of the body [and the life everlasting. Amen].

The last phrase is not found in the Latin text mentioned by Rufinus in 390.

This formula was used in the Church of Rome before the mid-second century AD. This text is extant in its Greek and Latin form; perhaps the Greek is the original. The Greek text was transmitted to us from Marcellus of Ancyra in the fourth century. As for the Latin text, it was transmitted to us from Rufinus in about 390 AD, where he compares it with the canon used in his church in the ancient church of Aquileia.

This ancient and shorter creeds continued to be in use for a long time. We find it in England since about the time of the Norman Conquest. This shorter formula remains preserved in the English Museum manuscripts.

2) *Current Creed*

> I believe in God, the Father almighty, creator of heaven and earth. I believe in Jesus Christ, God's only Son, our Lord, who was conceived by the Holy Spirit, born of the Virgin Mary, suffered under Potius Pilate, was crucified, died, and was buried; he descended to the dead. On the third day he rose again; he ascended into heaven, he is seated at the right hand of the Father, and he will come again to judge the living and the dead. I believe in the Holy Spirit, the holy catholic church, the communion of saints, the forgiveness of sins, the resurrection of the body, and the life everlasting. Amen.

There is much uncertainty regarding the date of the current creed. There were many additions made to it at different times, although some are very ancient. For example, "Creator of heaven and earth," first appeared in the text found in southern France dating to around 650 AD, although similar expressions were found in older texts. Also, "descended to Hades," is first found in the text mentioned by Rufinus, as part of the *Creed of Faith* of the church of Aquileia.

It is known that this canon took its current shape, perhaps without the phrases mentioned, plus "the communion of saints," in the era of Faustus of Reiz around 460 AD. From there, it became widespread until it reached Ireland, as it would seem, before the end of between the Eastern Orthodox traditions of the Coptic, Syriac, and Byzantine (Greek) rites.[29]

---

[29] Burmester, O. H. E. *The Egyptian of Coptic Church*. (Cairo: Coptic Society of Archeology, 1967), 327.

Greek Text	Syriac Text	Coptic Text
I believe	We believe	
All things visible	All things visible	Things visible
And in One Lord		We believe in One Lord
He came down from the heavens	He came down from heaven	
And was incarnate		Incarnated[30]
And of the Virgin Mary	And of the Virgin Mary the Pure and Mother of God	And of the Virgin Mary
Suffered and was buried	Suffered, died, and was buried	Suffered and was buried
And rose	And rose	And rose from the dead
According to the scriptures	According to his will	According to the scriptures
He sat on the right hand of the Father		He sat on the right hand of his Father
And will also come in glory	And will also come in great glory	And will also come in his glory
And in the Holy Spirit	And we believe in the Holy Spirit	Indeed, we believe in the Holy Spirit
The Lord and giver of life	The Lord and giver of life of all	The Lord and giver of life
We worship him and glorify him	To him is due worship and is glorified	We worship him and glorify him
Who spoke in the prophets	Who spoke in the prophets and apostles[31]	Who spoke in the prophets
Holy catholic and apostolic	Catholic holy apostolic	Holy catholic and apostolic
I confess one baptism	We acknowledge one baptism	We confess one baptism
I look for the resurrection of the dead	We hope for the resurrection of the dead	We look for the resurrection of the dead
And the life of the age to come	And the new life of the world to come	And the life of the age to come

---

30 The Coptic text of the canon does not include "and" and it directly mentions ⲁϥϭⲓⲥⲁⲣⲝ. The Arabic translation, however, adds "and" except in the Holy *Euchologion (1902)*, and the current Agpeya versions.

As for the Western churches, they added the phrase "and the Son," to the expression, "proceeds from the Father," such that it became, "Who proceeds from the Father and the Son." According to Schaff:

> There seems little doubt that the words were first inserted in Spain. As early as the year 400... and at Rome nothing of the kind was known... However, there can be no doubt that its introduction spread very rapidly through the West and that before long it was received practically everywhere except at Rome. In 809, Pope, Leo III... opposed the insertion of the Filioque... So firmly resolved was the Pope that the clause should not be introduced into the creed that he presented two silver shields to the *Confessio* in St. Peter's at Rome, on one of which was engraved the creed in Latin and on the other in Greek, without the addition... It was not till 1014 that for the first time the interpolated creed was used at mass with the sanction of the Pope. In that year Benedict VIII acceded to the urgent request of Henry II of Germany and so the papal authority was forced to yield, and the silver shields have disappeared from St. Peter's.[32]

Delayed Recitation of the Creed of Faith within the Eucharist

The Nicene-Constantinopolitan Creed is recited before the Eucharistic prayer in all the liturgies of the Eastern churches. In the churches of Jerusalem, Alexandria, and Antioch, it is recited before the holy kiss; in the Byzantine Church it is recited after the holy kiss. Armenians recite it immediately after the Gospel

---

[31] The Maronite Rite is in agreement with the Syriac Rite regarding this addition.
[32] *NPNF2-14*, 237-238.

according to the tradition of the Latin church.[33] For the Assyrians (the Eastern Syriacs), its recitation is before placing the oblations on the altar.

The Church of Rome also uses the Nicene-Constantinopolitan Creed in its daily services, especially the evening service. However, it uses the Apostles' Creed for Sundays and Feasts.

The habit of reciting the creed within the Eucharist in the Christian East was relatively late, that is, at the beginning of the sixth century. Before then, the creed occupied a special position in the sacrament of baptism (as we have mentioned). Nevertheless, James of Edessa (633-708 AD) mentions that its recitation in the Antiochian-Syrian Church began following the Nicene Council, that is, in the first half of the fourth century.[34] As for the West, the creed was recited in the Church of Rome, after Pope Benedict VIII (1012-1034) ordered its recitation in 1014.[35] The churches of Spain and Gaul had preceded the Church of Rome before this by some time.

The creed was integrated within the Eucharistic gatherings because they were truly a meeting of believers who hold the upright faith, having been renewed by the water and Spirit and anointed with the Myron by the hands of the Highest. The early church

---

[33] Brightman, F. E. *Liturgies Eastern and Western*. Vol. I., (Oxford: Clarendon Press, 1896), 426.
[34] Cf. Ignatius Aphrem II, *The Evident Investigations in the Eastern and Western Liturgies (al-Mabāḥth al-jaleya fī al-līturjiat al-sharqīa wa al-gharbeya)*, vol. 1, (Deir Al-Sharfa, 1924), 239.
[35] *ODCC*, (2nd Edition), 358.

believed that the unity of faith within the congregation is inevitable. Integrating the *Creed of Faith* in the Divine Liturgy is a clear indication of the indissoluble link between the unity of faith and the church. This connection was at the crux of the liturgical experience of the early church.

Unity of Church in Faith and Love, a Condition for Fulfilling the Eucharistic Ministry

The unity of faith along with the unity of love became a basic condition for church unity, and for completing the Eucharistic ministry in her. The Orthodox Church continues to observe this essential condition. It is not permitted for an unorthodox to approach communion in an Orthodox Church. Vice-versa, an Orthodox person is forbidden from communicating from mysteries offered by a non-Orthodox. This truth, of which we speak, is none other but the genuine experience of the Eucharist, which is broken for unity. It is, to put it in other words, the mystery of the church as expressed by Ignatius of Antioch (35-107 AD): "It is unity in faith and love."[36]

Our discussion leads us to the subject of church unity and Christian unity, which is a pressing issue today, more so than in the past. The difference between yesterday's unity, and the one we seek today, is vast. There is a clear deviation in our original faith, which was built on the tenets of unity.

---

[36] Epistle to the Philadelphians 2.6,4; Epistle to the Ephesians 4.2, 14.1, 20.2; Epistle to the Magnesians 1.2.

The Rite of Reciting the Creed of Faith in the Coptic Tradition

I previously mentioned that the *Liturgy of the Believers* is preceded by three prayers: the *Prayer of the Veil* (recited inaudibly by the priest before the altar veil), the *Three Great Litanies* (the priest recites audibly at the altar), and the *Reconciliation Prayer* (the prayer before the Anaphora).

In the Coptic rite, the creed is recited and the washing of the priest's hands occurs between the end of the *Three Great Litanies* and the beginning of the *Reconciliation Prayer*. The Antiochian-Syrian Church agrees with the Coptic Church in that the priest washes his hands immediately after the creed,[37] noting that the Syriac Church does not recite the litanies before the *Reconciliation Prayer*, which is called in the Syriac Church today the "prayer of peace,"[38] or, the "prayer of the kiss of peace."

The catechumens were not permitted to recite the creed in church since they had not yet been baptized. In this regard, Gregory the Theologian (329-389) says:

> ... if to the low, are not reserved enough, for they commit pearls to clay, and the noise of thunder to weak ears, and the sun to feeble eyes, and solid food to those who are still using milk; whereas they ought to lead them little by little up to what lies beyond them, and to bring them up to the

---

[37] Brightman, *op. cit.*, 84.
[38] This expression is known in the Coptic Church since the sixth century, as evident from Canon 97 of the Church Canons attributed to Basil the Great.

higher truth; adding light to light, and supplying truth upon truth.
(Oration 41.6)

The creed is preceded in the Coptic rite by the call of the deacon saying, in Greek:

> Ἐν σοφίᾳ Θεοῦ πρόσχωμεν. Κύριε ἐλέησον, Κύριε ἐλέησον.
>
> In the wisdom of God let us attend. Lord have mercy. Lord have mercy.

This exact response is found in the Syriac rite in the *Liturgy of James the Brother of the Lord*. It is also found in the Byzantine rite, in the *Liturgy of John Chrysostom* (347-407), but without the word "God" and "Lord Have Mercy" in both instances. Thus, the response in both liturgies is: "In wisdom, let us attend."[39]

This response, is recorded by Ibn Sebāʿ as:

> In God's wisdom respond.

Then he adds:

> **Then the congregation say the true Orthodox creed,** word by word, all with one voice, in its entirety…[40]

---

[39] Brightman, *op. cit.*, 42, 383; Burmester, O.H.E. *The Greek Kirugmatat, Versicles and Responses, and Hymns in the Coptic Liturgy*, OCP Vol II, N. 3-4, Roma 1936, 374.

[40] Yoḥanna Ibn A'bī Zakaria Ibn Sebāʿ. *Book of the Precious Jewel in Church Sciences (Ketāb al-Jawhara al-Nafīsa Fī 'Oloum al-Kanīsa)*. Arabic. (Cairo: New Cairo Printing House, 1966), 215.

As for Ibn Kabar (d. 1324), he mentioned the deacon's response in Arabic and Greek in Coptic letters as follows:

> In wisdom of God respond[41]
> Ἐν ⲥⲟⲫⲓⲁ☐ Ⲑⲉⲟⲩ ⲡⲣⲟⲥⲭⲱⲙⲉⲛ.

Then Ibn Kabar continues:

> **And the congregation say the entire Creed,** except in the Covenant Thursday and Bright Saturday Liturgies, as will be mentioned in due place.[42]

As for the Vatican Manuscript No. 17 (Coptic) of 1288 CE, it says, "The congregation say the Orthodox Creed," without mentioning the deacon's response. I have previously mentioned that this is the oldest **complete** Coptic-Arabic Euchologion known to this day.

The Oxford Manuscript No. 360 (Huntington), which is slightly older than the Vatican Manuscript No. 17 (Coptic), states as follows:

> The deacon says: In the wisdom of God listen. **The congregation says, 'We believe in one God.**

---

[41] The Greek word (Proskomen), which was transferred verbatim to the Coptic, stems from (Proseeko), that is: "listen," and not "respond." But Ibn Kabar repeats this again, using the same word, in the deacon's response which precedes the Cherubic Praise.

[42] Shams al-Ri'āsa Abū al-Barakāt, *The Lamp of Darkness and the Clarification of the Service (Miṣbāḥ al-ẓulma wa 'īdāḥ al-khidma)*, vol. 1, Library of al-Karouz, 1971, verified by Samir Khalil the Jesuit, Chapter 17, Folio 206v.

Pope Gabriāl V (1409-1427) affirms that the congregation are the ones who say the Creed, by briefly saying:

While they say the Creed, the priest washes his hands…[43]

This is also what is mentioned by the Euchologion manuscripts in the Library of the Monastery of Macarius.

In Manuscripts No. 133 and 134 (Rites), we read:

Then they say the Creed with caution.

Manuscript No. 136 (Rites) states:

The congregation says the Creed.

Manuscript No. 147 states:

The deacon says ˙Ncoφia⸱ then **the congregation says the Creed.**

In Euchologion (1902), the deacon's response was inserted with the Greek pronunciation previously mentioned, appended by a Coptic word, "ϧen oυmeθmhi," that is, "in truth." Then he adds: "**The congregation says the Orthodox Creed.**"[44]

---

[43] Pope Gabriāl V, *Ritual Order*, Published by A'lfūns ʿAbd Allah the Franciscan. (Cairo: The Franciscan Center for Oriental Christian Studies, 1964), 76.

[44] I have included a thorough explanation for the Creed in the book of *The Agpeya, the Prayers of the Hours*. It was also mentioned in *Baptism of Water and Spirit*.

Perhaps the reader might wonder at such an extensive explanation over a given that Copts grew up with in their churches, that is, that the congregation recites the Creed together in one voice. The *Book of the Service of Deacons and Hymns*, in its various editions, being the book reviewed by Hegumen ʿAbd al-Massīh Salīb al-Massʿūdī al-Baramūsī, mentions in its fourth publication:

> The deacon says, addressing the congregation: "listen in the wisdom of God, Lord have mercy, Lord have mercy, truly."

Then adds:

> "Then one serving deacon stands at the door of the altar, facing West, flanked by two deacons holding candles who recite the following Creed in Coptic, **while the congregation is silent,** until they end at 'for the remission of sins,' **at which point all the deacons and congregation recite the last part.**[45] Then another deacon comes forward who recites the Creed in Arabic, and at its conclusion, all the deacons chant "Amen." **As for the congregation, they recite the Creed inaudibly with the translating deacon.**"

We shall not overlook what was mentioned. The Copts were not keen to document their rites, which encouraged me to search into every word in any book or manuscript or any reference which was ignored. How many doors were flung wide open when I discovered a word in a footnote or a passing ritual remark.

---

[45] The last part is chanted in Coptic: "And we look for the resurrection of the dead and the life of the age to come. Amen."

What is mentioned in the *Book of the Service of the Deacons and Hymns* is summarized as:

- It is the first source to refer to the rite of reciting the creed in Coptic, then translating it into Arabic.

- The congregation does not participate in reciting the creed, but it is recited by the deacons standing at the door of the altar facing the congregation, whether in Coptic or Arabic. The congregation participate in the last phrase only.

By comparing what has been mentioned with what the deacon says immediately before this, which includes the word "let us attend," or "listen" –as mentioned in the manuscripts– it becomes clear that the response does mean that the congregation is to listen, not to participate. What further clarifies the matter, is that in the Byzantine rite, which contains the same deacon's response as in the Coptic, the Creed is recited by the officiating priest, not the congregation.

In the *Liturgy of John Chrysostom*, we read:

> The deacon shouts: the doors, the doors. In wisdom let us listen. And the celebrant says: I believe in one God...

The difficulty arises from the inaccessibility of a Euchologion manuscript that refers to the rite of reciting the creed, before the thirteenth century, being the time in which the first double columned Coptic-Arabic Euchologion manuscript appeared.

It was imperative for the person documenting what was mentioned in the *Book of the Service of Deacons and Hymns*-being the only book that mentioned the congregation's refraining from reciting the Creed, contrary to all the known sources and manuscripts- to cite or reference this information. But this was not done.

In all that was mentioned, there was not one ritual remark about a deacon holding up a cross during the call that precedes the recitation of the creed. Presbyter Samʿān Ibn Kalīl's (twelfth century) says in the *Wisdom of the Egyptian Fathers*:

> The deacon holds the honorable cross, and raises it, calling out to the congregation: 'Listen in the wisdom of God, Lord have mercy, Lord have mercy,' and he continues standing in his place until the congregation concludes reciting the Creed." His words, "Lord have mercy," are a plea for God to forbid, through His mercy, the unorthodoxy of the heart, that makes those who recite the Creed recite it with their mouths only, not with their hearts. Therefore, he raises up the cross, so that none resemble Judas, of whom Isaiah said, "This people honor me with their lips, but their hearts are far away from me." Isaiah said this because the people of old were well versed in recitation, but not in piety. He lifts up the cross, modelling the bronze serpent uplifted by Moses, to which all who looked received healing. Let us receive healing by an upright recitation of the Creed, and through the sign of wisdom and life which belongs to our Lord Jesus Christ, the honorable cross. Know that you are clever and wise through the grace of the Holy Spirit, and that you, in all cases, do not fully comprehend the might of the words of the Creed a true understanding, if the wisdom of the cross does not dwell in your conscience, and remains as if before you continually... therefore, memorize the words of the Creed, and repeat them whenever the waves

of false wisdom rise, and cling to the sign of the hope of life, the cross of our Lord Jesus Christ.[46]

Second: The Priest Washing His Hands

Introduction

In the Holy Bible, washing with water was either for personal purity or ritual cleansing. The regular washings in the Old or New Testaments refer specifically to washing the feet,[47] hands,[48] and face.[49]

In the Old Testament, the priests and Levites were to wash with water for ritual cleansing, before performing their commissioned tasks, lest they die.[50] In the Old Testament, the priest did not wear shoes during his assigned service. When the priests of Israel ascended to the service before the Ark of the Covenant, either in the tabernacle of meeting, or in the temple, or the synagogue (thereafter) to bless the people, they ascended barefoot. It was not permitted for anyone to walk on the temple ground wearing shoes, or with dirty feet, therefore, there was a need for the laver for washing the feet.[51]

---

[46] Presbyter Samʿān Ibn Kalīl, *Meanings of signing the Sign of the Cross (Mʿaānī Rashm al-Ṣalīb). On Spiritual Life and the Rites of the Coptic Orthodox Church. (c. Twelfth-Century)*, 72-73.
[47] Genesis 18.4, 19.2, 24.32, 43.24; John 13.3-19
[48] Exodus 30.19,21; Matthew 15.2
[49] Genesis 43.31; Matthew 6.17
[50] Exodus 30.20
[51] Jews today do not walk barefoot during their service but wear a type of stocking. Many Jews currently remove their shoes and walk barefoot during the Day of Atonement, and on the ninth of Abib.

Ibn Sebā' (thirteenth century) says:

> ... as the church is analogous to the dome of time... there must be in the church a bronze laver with water, to wash the feet of all who ascend to the altar of God...[52]

Hand Washing in the Various Rites

The Coptic, Syriac,[53] and Armenian rites practice the washing of the hands following the creed and before the holy kiss. In the Byzantine rite, the ritual of washing the hands is only at the offering. In this regard, the Coptic rite is distinct in that the priest washes his hands twice, firstly at the offering of the lamb, and secondly after the creed during the Divine Liturgy.

The ancient rite of the Church of Jerusalem states that the deacon is the one who carries the pitcher for washing the hands of the priest, as Cyril of Jerusalem (315-386) mentions.[54]

Priest Hand Washing in the Coptic Rite

Book VIII of the Apostolic Constitutions writes concerning this:

> Then let a Sub-Deacon bring water to wash the hands of the Priests, which is a symbol of the purity of souls devoted to God.[55]

---

[52] Yoḥanna Ibn A'bī Zakaria Ibn Sebā', *op. cit.*, 177.
[53] Brightman, *op. cit.*, 82.
[54] *NPNF2-7*, 292 (Catechetical Letter 23.2).
[55] Warren, Frederick Edward. *Liturgy and Ritual of the Ante-Nicene Church.* (London: S.P.C.K., 1912), 290.

(Apostolic Constitutions 8.11.12)

This text is analogous to that of the Coptic Apostolic Canons:

> And let a subdeacon bring water that the priests may wash their hands for a sign of the purity of their souls dedicated to the almighty God.[56]
> (Coptic Apostolic Canons 1.52.13)

Athanasius of Alexandria (328-373) says:

> We are to be prepared, to approach the heavenly Lamb, and to touch the heavenly food, therefore, let us wash our hands and purify the body, and keep the mind from any evil.[57]

Presbyter Samʿān Ibn Kalīl in the twelfth century makes an clever testimony to the meaning of the priest washing his hands before beginning the Divine Liturgy:

> The priest washes his hands, not because he emulates the Roman governor who crucified our Lord, but rather that Pilate, the governor, wanted to emulate the righteous, so he washed his hands, declaring His innocence, being a hypocrite. The priest recites the psalm: 'Purge me with Your hyssop and I shall be clean, wash me and I shall be whiter than snow...' requesting the purity of his soul, and not because the water gives purity (it is lifeless), but washing moves the soul to seek purity from the Holy Spirit who dwells in the soul and body since baptism.[58]

Here it is clear, that until the twelfth century, washing the hands had dual functions in (1) preparing

---

[56] Brightman, *op. cit.*, 462.
[57] Athanasius of Alexandria, *Festal Epistle V*
[58] Presbyter Samʿān Ibn Kalīl, *op. cit.*, 74.

the priest to bear the Holy Body on his hands for sanctification (as is the common ritual in all the East),[59] and (2) in spiritually moving the heart of the priest to request from the Lord purity of his heart, soul, and body through the fire of the Holy Spirit who dwells in him since baptism.

In the thirteenth and fourteenth century, washing the hands was commonly known as a means of preparing the priest for bearing the Holy Body for sanctification.

For Ibn Sebā', the priest washes his hands for sanctifying the oblations.[60]

For Ibn Kabar,

> The water is offered to the priest, to wash his hands, and from that point, he does not touch anything except the consecrated altar vessels only.[61]

Dionysius the Areopagite mentions that if the high priest prepares to wash his hands, the priests stand in order and wash their hands individually according to their ranks. Thus, the goal of washing the hands is to sanctify oneself for the liturgical service, rather than

---

[59] I explained this point in discussing the rite of Offering of the Lamb.
[60] Yoḥanna Ibn A'bī Zakaria Ibn Sebā', *op. cit.*, 217.
[61] Shams al-Ri'āsa Abū al-Barakāt, *The Lamp of Darkness and the Clarification of the Service (Miṣbāḥ al-ẓulma wa 'īdāḥ al-khidma)*, vol. 1, *op. cit.*, Chapter 17. The Vatican Manuscript No. 17 (Coptic) and Oxford Manuscript No. 360 (Huntington) do not mention the priest washing his hands after the Creed of Faith.

being a (false) symbol of the priest's unaccountability of the congregation's sins.

In the Middle Ages, a new interpretation appeared that skewed the meaning of washing the hands. The new meaning denotes that the priest is no longer held accountable of anyone who approaches the communion unworthily! In this regard, Pope Gabriāl V (1409-1427) says:

> When they chant the Creed, the priest washes his hands at the north side of the altar three times. He looks towards the west and sprinkles his hands before all the people, that is, he warns them to watch over their souls before communion. He is innocent of anyone who dares and partakes of the Body and Blood of Christ unworthily, receiving what Judas Iscariot received when he partook of the Body and Blood of Christ, being unworthy. Satan encompassed and dwelt in him, until he made him sell his Master, handing Him to the accursed Jews who crucified Him. God save us from temptations. Then he dries them with a clean towel.[62]

---

[62] Pope Gabriāl V, *op. cit.*, 76. The Monastery of Macarius Manuscript No. 134 (Rites) from the eighteenth century, arranged by Bishop Michael of Samanoud, mentions: "… the priest washes his hands three times, and before drying them, he turns towards the congregation and shakes his hands of water before them, being innocent of their iniquities, then he dries his hands well…" This is also what is described in the *Trinitarian Mystery in Pastoral Care* by one church teacher from the middle ages, where he links between Pilate washing his hands to be innocent of the blood of Christ, and the priest washing his hands to be innocent of the faults of the people! This is an erroneous explanation to the meaning of this ritual, depriving it of its spiritual and liturgical meaning.
There is a vast difference between what Pilate did while washing his hands, and what the priest says when he washes his hands.

This is similar to what Hegumen ʿAbd al-Massīh Salīb al-Massʿūdī al-Baramūsī mentions in *Euchologion* (1902), citing Pope Gabriāl V:

> While reciting the Creed, the priest washes his hands... on themselves before communion.[63] **And disavows himself of anyone who dares to take communion unworthily without his knowledge.** Then he dries his hands with a clean towel.[64]

This understanding spread among many, after it found its way into the printing press with the publication of the *Holy Euchologion*. The genuine understanding of the washing of the hands was unfortunately lost. Nevertheless, we still have the prayers recited by the priest while washing his hands, which have no connection with what appeared in the Middle Ages.

Perhaps the primary principles to this notion, which appeared in the Coptic Church in the Middle Ages, is what was mentioned in Deuteronomy 21.1-9:

> If, in the land that the Lord your God is giving you to possess, a body is found lying in open country, and it is not

---

The priest prays during this a prayer specific to him personally, having no connection to disavowing responsibility for the faults of others. He says, "Purge me with Your hyssop and I shall be clean, wash me and I shall be whiter than snow. Make me to hear joy and gladness so my bones may rejoice. I wash my hands in purity and go about your altar O Lord, to hear the voice of your praise. Alleluia."

[63] Until this sentence, Hegumen ʿAbd al-Massīh Salīb al-Massʿūdī al-Baramūsī copies the text as mentioned by Pope Gabriāl V.

[64] *Euchologion (1902)*, 296.

known who struck the person down, then your elders and your judges shall come out to measure the distances to the towns that are near the body. The elders of the town nearest the body shall take a heifer that has never been worked, one that has not pulled in the yoke; the elders of that town shall bring the heifer down to a wadi with running water, which is neither plowed nor sown, and shall break the heifer's neck there in the wadi. Then the priests, the sons of Levi, shall come forward, for the Lord your God has chosen them to minister to him and to pronounce blessings in the name of the Lord, and by their decision all cases of dispute and assault shall be settled. All the elders of that town nearest the body shall wash their hands over the heifer whose neck was broken in the wadi, and they shall declare: "Our hands did not shed this blood, nor were we witnesses to it. Absolve, O Lord, your people Israel, whom you redeemed; do not let the guilt of innocent blood remain in the midst of your people Israel." Then they will be absolved of bloodguilt. So you shall purge the guilt of innocent blood from your midst, because you must do what is right in the sight of the Lord.
(Deuteronomy 21.1-9)

Thus, washing the hands with water was to deny the responsibility for innocent bloodshed. But this proclamation is accompanied by a quote said during this practice, to confirm its meaning or symbolism:

> Our hands did not shed this blood, nor were we witnesses to it.

Washing the hands for liberty from guilt was a Jewish practice, as it was a Greek practice, and likewise Roman. Yet, this liberty from guilt was one of many meanings pertaining to the Jewish ritual of washing the hands. The Talmud contains chapters on purification, washing and bathing. One of those chapters consists of four sections, all pertaining to the washing of hands.

Also, in the sayings of Samuel the Prophet to the elders of Bethlehem: "Sanctify yourselves, and come with me to the sacrifice."[65] *"Sanctify"* denotes the washings that precede offering a sacrifice, and not disavowing responsibility.

The habit of washing the hands was transferred to the Christian church, especially in the Christian Eucharist. However, it was not transferred with the Jewish or gentile notion of disavowing. The priest in the New Testament caries on his shoulders the sins of the congregation whom he serves, along with his sin. He approaches the heavenly altar, to take, for himself, and for his congregation, justification through the blood of Christ which purifies from all sins.

The priest asks for himself, and for the people, saying,

> We ask and entreat Your goodness, O Lover of Mankind, that, since **You have purified us all**, You join us to Yourself through **our partaking** of Your divine Mysteries, that we may become **filled** with Your Holy Spirit.[66]

The priest does not disavow the sin of the congregation, but asks for himself, that his sin may not be a hindrance to the work of the Holy Spirit in the people whom he serves. He says:

---

[65] 1 Samuel 16.5
[66] H G Bishop Serapion, and H G Bishop Youssef. *The Divine Liturgies: The Anaphoras of Saints Basil, Gregory, and Cyril*. 2nd Edition., (Dallas: Coptic Orthodox Diocese of the Southern United States, 2007), 225.

> Because of my own sins and the abominations of my heart, deprive not Your people of the grace of Your Holy Spirit... Therefore, O Lord, let Your servants, my fathers and my brethren and my own weakness, be absolved by my mouth, through Your Holy Spirit.[67]

Here the priest pleas before the Lord to forgive the sins of the congregation, not disavowing himself from their sins.

As for the person who partakes of communion from the Divine Mysteries, unworthily and without repentance, bears his own faults, as Paul the Apostle says: *"let a man examine himself,"*[68] and, *"For he who eats and drinks in an unworthy manner eats and drinks **judgment** to himself, not discerning the Lord's body."*[69] Judgment befalls the soul of the one who approaches communion unworthily and not on the priest who gives them the Divine Mysteries.

The Coptic Church continued, until the end of the nineteenth century, to highly esteem the significance of the ritual of washing the hands and did not view it as a means of disavowing. Alfred Butler, who visited the churches of Old Cairo in the end of the nineteenth century, reports to us what he saw:

> For the congregation, the creed is repeated by all together; whereupon the priest washes his hands thrice, and turning round wrings them dry before the people.[70]

---

[67] *Ibid.*, 228, 227.
[68] 1 Corinthians 11.28
[69] 1 Corinthians 11.29
[70] Butler, Alfred J. *The Ancient Coptic Churches of Egypt.* (Oxford: Clarendon Press, 1884.), 287.

The priest washing his hands and drying them before the people, signifies that the deacon brought the water to the priest at the north end of the altar as mentioned in the ancient rites. There is no indication, however, to what Pope Gabriāl V said:

> ... sprinkles his hands before all the people.

THE RECONCILIATION PRAYER AND THE KISS OF PEACE

First: Reconciliation Prayer

Introduction

The *Reconciliation Prayer* is known as the *pro-anaphoral portion* (Prayer before the anaphora). As for the word *Anaphora* (ἡ ἀναφορά), it means to *lift up* or *offer*. *Anaphora* refers to the main body of the Eucharistic prayer, the part containing the sanctification, the commemoration, and the communion. Therefore, the word encompasses most of the liturgical prayers, and as such, it is applied generally to the offering of the Eucharist.[71]

Anaphora for Syrians and Maronites is equivalent to *Qudas* (liturgy) for Copts. For the Assyrians is it called *Qadasho*. The oldest known anaphora is the *Apostolic Tradition of Hippolytus*, transcribed before 235 CE. It is perceived as a sample and not a complete or the standard anaphora. In the early church, the priest offered *thanksgiving* to God to the best of his ability. However, the priests did resort to a few samples of anaphoras for prayer.[72]

---

[71] Smith and Cheetham, *op. cit*, 80.
[72] Dix, *op. cit.*, 6.

Shortly thereafter, the ecumenical councils forbade these improvised prayers, lest heresies become integrated within the liturgical texts.

The *Reconciliation Prayer*, or the *Prayer before the Anaphora* is also known in the ancient Coptic rite as the *Prayer of the Holy Kiss*,[73] or the *Prayer of Kissing the Father*,[74] or the *Prayer of the Kiss*.[75] In the Antiochian-Syriac rite, it is known as the *Prayer of Peace* or the *Prayer of the Kiss of Peace*.[76]

In the Antiochian-Syrian Church, the priest ascends to the height of the altar and stands to the side of the table of life, facing East, and begins the *Prayer of Peace* to reconcile humans with God. Peace is exchanged between the faithful in the church after the priest is blessed by the mysteries. The deacon carries this peace and bring it to the faithful, and they greet each other with a holy kiss or through the well-renowned ecclesial greeting.[77]

Reconciliation Prayer in the Coptic Rite

The *Reconciliation Prayer* is known by all the various rites as the prayer before announcing the *Kiss of*

---

[73] Cf. Yoḥanna Ibn A'bī Zakaria Ibn Sebā', *op. cit.*, 216.
[74] Cf. Vatican Manuscript No. 17.
[75] Cf. Oxford Manuscript No. 360 (Huntington).
[76] Here the relationship between the Reconciliation Prayer and the Kiss of Peace (which immediately follows) becomes clear. This reminds us of the ancient call by the deacon that any who have something against his brother in their heart should refrain from communion.
[77] Patriarchal Magazine, No. 138, 1994, 529.

Peace. All the rites begin this prayer with the priest addressing the congregation: "Peace with all," "Peace to everyone," "Peace to all of you, "Peace of God be with you all,"[78] or "Peace with you." The congregation responds: "and with your spirit," or "to your spirit."

Cyril of Alexandria (412-444) says:

> The rite in the church since the beginning, used at the beginning of all services and sacraments is "Peace be with you all," and the response is, "and with your spirit." As Christ used to say it to His disciples always, He made it thus a rule for the entire church.

In the Coptic rite, the priest approaches the altar to pray the *Reconciliation Prayer* with bare hands, being like Adam who was expelled naked from Paradise. But, after the reconciliation, he places the veils on his hands, because he has been clothed with grace and became worthy to stand before our Lord Jesus Christ, by His death and resurrection.[79]

When the priest begins the *Reconciliation Prayer*, a deacon stands before him and lifts up the honourable cross saying, "Pray for perfect peace..." The deacon warns the congregation to accept any other peace but the peace of our Lord Jesus Christ who died for us, had compassion on our fallen race, and raised us from death by his life-giving death. The deacon lifts up the cross

---

[78] As in the *Apostolic Constitutions*, and the liturgy of the Church of Rome (with a slight variation).
[79] Presbyter Samʿān Ibn Kalīl, *op. cit.*, 74-75.

with strength, not with laxity, as he saves by his mighty service.[80]

In the *Reconciliation Prayer*, the priest takes the triangular veil placed over the covering (prospherein), and holds it between his hands while saying,

> According to Your good will, O God, fill our hearts with Your peace…

The triangular veil represents the seal on the tomb of our Saviour. Lifting this veil denotes breaking the seal on the tomb, in anticipation of lifting up the covering (prospherein), a symbol of the resurrection during the Kiss of Peace. During this period, the deacon stands in his ancient traditional place, before the priest, and lifts up the cross.

Prayers of Reconciliation in Coptic Liturgies

There is more than one *Reconciliation Prayer* in the liturgies of the Church of Alexandria. All of them were borrowed from the Cappadocian or Syriac rite.

According to the Euchologion (1902), there are two Reconciliation Prayers in the three Coptic Liturgies.

In the *Liturgy of Basil*, there are two *Reconciliation Prayers*: 1) "O God, the Great, the Eternal, who formed man in incorruption," by Basil the Great (330-379), and 2) "Exalted above all the power of speech and all the

---

[80] *Ibid.*

thoughts of the mind is the richness of Your gifts, O our Master," by John of Bostra (Syria/650 CE).

The Oxford Manuscript No. 360 (Huntington) has two additional *Reconciliation Prayers* in Coptic and Arabic. They are as follows:

Reconciliation Prayer according to the Oxford Manuscript No. 360 (Huntington)

> O God, the maker of everything, more so humans who You created speaking in Your image. You brought him to the universe and adorned him with holy endowments. Who gave us the law of love for each other, wanting for all to be one, as You are one, You and Your only-begotten Son, our Lord, God, and Saviour Jesus Christ. You also, our Master, make us free from all separation. Make our hearts one in fellowship and unity of Your Holy Spirit. Make us worthy to greet one another with a holy kiss, having become one body and one spirit, as we were called with one hope to call upon you, through Christ Jesus. Through Whom…

Another Reconciliation Prayer according to the Oxford Manuscript No. 360 (Huntington)

> God, the Master of all, make us worthy of this salvation, this of which we the unworthy O Philanthropic one, so that if You purify us all of all filth, and all deception, and all hypocrisy, we become worthy to greet one another with a holy kiss, having become one body and one spirit, through the bonds of love and peace of our Lord Jesus Christ, with whom You are blessed, with the Holy life-giving Spirit, equal with you, now and forever…

In the *Coptic Liturgy of Gregory*, there are two Reconciliation Prayers: 1) "O You, The Being, who is and who abides forever," by Gregory of Nazianzus (329-

389), and 2) "O Christ our God, the fearful," by Severus of Antioch (465-538).

In the *Liturgy of Cyril (Mark)*, there are two Reconciliation Prayers: 1) "O Author of life and King of the ages," by Severus of Antioch (465-538), and 2) "O God of love and giver of the oneness of heart," by John of Bostra (Syria/650 CE).

Commentary on Some Reconciliation Prayers in the Coptic Liturgy

- All the *Reconciliation Prayers* are supplication prayers for the Lord to grant us heavenly peace and divine love to make us worthy to greet one another with a holy kiss without hypocrisy.

- The *Reconciliation Prayer* declares the reconciliation of the Father with humanity and the filling of the earth with the peace coming down to us from heaven, through the incarnation, death, and resurrection of the only-begotten Son Jesus Christ. It asks the Father to make us worthy to greet one another with a holy kiss, to approach the Holy and share in the Holies with love. This love for which the church sets aside a special call for prayer: "Pray for… love,"[81] so that the commandment of the Holy Bible be fulfilled in us: "*Since you have purified your souls in obeying the truth through the Spirit in sincere love of*

---

[81] H G Bishop Serapion, and H G Bishop Youssef., *op. cit.*, 175.

the brethren, love one another fervently with a pure heart."[82]

Before the deacon announces, "Greet one another...,"[83] he recites the response of the *Reconciliation Prayer*, "Pray for... the holy apostolic kisses."[84] When the whole church prays to the Lord to make their greeting holy apostolic kiss, then the deacon cries out saying, "Greet one another with a holy kiss..." Here the focus is on the importance of praying for the holy kiss, to be without deceit or hypocrisy before exchanging the kiss.

> Approaching the holy place is very fearsome. It is written that our God is a consuming fire. Our God is not like the fire of this world, my beloved, but this the Holy Spirit has taught us. He, as the fire on which you place a veil cannot but be burned, likewise the sinners who want to cling to God while dwelling in their sins, they will perish like the veil burned by the fire.
> (Canon 76 of Athanasius II, Patriarch of Alexandria)

- For the *Reconciliation Prayer* to begin by reciting the history of salvation, beginning with the creation and fall, was not a general rule applied to all the prayers. This account only applies to the first *Reconciliation Prayers* found in the *Liturgy of Basil* and the *Liturgy of Gregory*.

- Most *Reconciliation Prayers*, however, mention the appearance of the second *hypostasis*, His incarnation and His becoming man, and filling the earth with

---

[82] 1 Peter 1.22
[83] H G Bishop Serapion, and H G Bishop Youssef., *op. cit.*, 177.
[84] *Ibid.*, 175.

heavenly peace. The *Reconciliation Prayer* in the *Liturgy of Cyril* is the one which focused on the core of this heavenly peace, calling it "the heavenly peace... full of salvation."[85]

> And make us worthy of the heavenly peace which befits Your divinity and is full of salvation, that we may give the same to one another in perfect love, and greet one another with a holy kiss... And cast us not behind, we Your servants, on account of the defilement of our sins... So make us worthy, O our Master, with a holy heart and a soul filled with Your grace, to stand before You and bring in unto You this holy sacrifice— which is rational, spiritual, and bloodless...[86]

This is the entryway to our fellowship in the Divine Liturgy. These are the two supports through which we draw closer to the Lord and stand in His presence: heavenly peace and heartfelt love. Through them we become worthy to greet one another.

Why did the *Reconciliation Prayer* emphasize these points, specifically? Rather, why was the *Reconciliation Prayer* articulated in such a manner? All the Early Christian writings agreed that the presence of one unworthy person at the holy Eucharist amid the congregation harms the whole church, and the effectiveness of the sacrifice itself!

The *Didache* says that it is the responsibility of those entering the fellowship of the Eucharist to watch over each other. They should not allow anyone in sin or dispute to approach communion since the partaking of

---

[85] H G Bishop Serapion, and H G Bishop Youssef., *op. cit.*, 329.
[86] H G Bishop Serapion, and H G Bishop Youssef., *op. cit.*, 329-330.

the impure also defiles the rest. The *Didache* warns, "that your sacrifice be not polluted."[87] Hence, the presence of the careless, negligent, or impure in the Divine Liturgy, and their fellowship in the holy sacrament, causes harm that affects all. From whence came the necessity of the community kiss, or the general reconciliation, as a necessary replacement for the public confession that the believers practiced in the early Christian era.

This does not imply that the Divine Liturgy was placed for saints only, otherwise, no one would dare approach the altar. However, it is for the penitent sinners who are constantly resisting the physical desires of their body, world, and Satan. Those are the ones who confess their sins and seek God's mercy.

- The heavenly peace chant uttered by the angels on the Lord Jesus's birth: "*Glory to God in the highest, and on earth peace, goodwill toward men!*"[88] is a chant known to all the various rites. In the Coptic rite, it is called the *Angelic Praise*, and the *Major Doxology* in the Byzantine rite. This chant became known in the Roman Liturgy late in about the sixth century.

- The first Reconciliation Prayer in the *Coptic Liturgy of Gregory*, says:

---

[87] Allen, G. C., trans. *The Didache: The Teachings of the Twelve Apostles*, (London: The Astolat Press, 1903), 9; Didache 14.2.
[88] Luke 2.14

O You, THE BEING, who were and who abide forever.	Ὁ ὢν, καὶ προὢν, καὶ διαμένων εἰς τοὺς αἰῶνας.
The co-eternal, co-essential, co-enthroned, and co-creator with the Father.	ὃ τῷ πατρὶ συναΐδιος καὶ ὁμοούσιος, καὶ σύνθρονος, καὶ συνδημιουργός ...

Second: The Holy Kiss

Introduction

The holy kiss is exchanged by the congregation upon the deacon's call, "Greet one another." This response, which begins with the call for the holy kiss is divided into three main segments.

The first segment of the response is "Greet one another with a holy kiss."[89] Upon this call, the people greet each other and chant the corresponding *Aspasmos Adam* of the day.

The second segment of the response is "Lord have mercy. Lord have mercy. Lord have mercy. Yea, Lord, who are Jesus Christ, the Son of God, hear us and have mercy upon us."[90] The deacon chants this segment at the conclusion of the *Aspasmos Adam*. The deacon lifts up the cross before the priest and then lifts up the

---

[89] H G Bishop Serapion, and H G Bishop Youssef., *op. cit.*, 177.
[90] *Ibid.*

covering (prospherein),[91] exposing the holies. This rite is according to the *Coptic Liturgy of Basil*.

The *Liturgy of Mark* does not include this second segment of the response, passing from the first segment directly to the third segment.[92]

In the *Liturgy of Gregory*, the second segment is:

> Let us stand well, let us stand reverently, let us stand earnestly, let us stand in peace, let us stand in the fear of God, with trembling and contrition.[93]

We find this second segment of the response in the liturgies of Jerusalem, Antioch, and Constantinople.[94] This segment belongs more to the Syriac than Coptic rite, although it is found in the *Coptic Liturgy of Gregory*, which does not follow the Egyptian Anaphora rite.

The third segment of the response is "Offer, [offer, offer] in order. Stand with trembling. Look towards the East. Let us attend."[95] This segment is the beginning of the anaphora, the centre of the Eucharistic Mystery. Therefore, it is chanted alone (without the other two segments) in all liturgies except the Eucharistic Liturgy. This segment is chanted in the

---

[91] *Pospherein* for Copts; *Shoshaf* for the Byzantines; and *Nafora* for the Syrians.
[92] H G Bishop Serapion, and H G Bishop Youssef., *op. cit.*, 331.
[93] *Ibid.*, 258.
[94] Ignatius Aphrem II, *op. cit.*, 244.
[95] *Ibid.*

Liturgy of the Laqan and the *Liturgy of the Consecration of the Myron and Galileon.*

The *Apostolic Constitutions* mentions looking toward the East:

> After this, let all rise up with one consent, and looking Eastward, after the departure of the catechumens and penitents, pray in the Eastward position to God who ascended up to the heaven of heavens, remembering also the original situation of paradise in the East, whence the first man was expelled, after he had broken the commandment, persuaded by the serpent's guile.[96]

Liturgical Meaning of the Holy Kiss

The holy kiss, ἀσπασμός, is an ancient liturgical practice accompanying the Divine Liturgy known since the early Christian eras.

The holy kiss is an inseparable part of the Christian Liturgy known in the universal church, East and West, except the Anglican Church of England.[97]

According to Gregory Dix, the holy kiss is the sign of love and fellowship among the one body of Christ, the church. In the Christian Church, the kiss,

> Was given to a newly consecrated bishop at his enthronement, not only by the clergy but by every confirmed member of his new church, before he offered the

---

[96] Warren, *op. cit.*, 309.
[97] Dix, *op. cit.*, 110.

eucharist sacrifice with them for the first time as their high priest.[98]

Subsequently, each bishop is to give this holy kiss to each newly baptized Christian, after baptism and confirmation with the Holy Myron.[99]

It was not permitted for those seeking baptism to exchange the kiss of peace with the believers because they have not yet become members in the one body of Christ and have not yet received the Holy Spirit. Therefore, someone seeking baptism cannot exchange the peace and love of Christ.[100]

In antiquity, the kiss of peace was exchanged between Jews as a sign of love and friendship, such as when Isaac kissed Jacob. The church inherited this practice from the Judaic tradition, but with a new meaning.[101]

During the days of our Lord Jesus Christ on earth, the kiss was the traditional welcome in any traditional Jewish meal, the lack of which deserved reproach and criticism.[102] Based on this, the kiss took its place in the Eucharistic meal in the first days in Jerusalem. Perhaps, it might have been practiced in the Lord's Supper.[103]

---

[98] *Ibid.*, 107.
[99] *Ibid.*, 107.
[100] *Ibid.*
[101] *Ibid.*
[102] Luke 7.45
[103] Dix, *op. cit.*, 107.

Paul the Apostle alluded to the holy kiss more than once as a symbol of Christian communion, but without a clear indication of its presence in the Eucharist. However, it is difficult to deny its absence in the Christian Eucharist.[104] From the early inception of the Christian Church, church unity in the one body of Christ[105] was the essence of the Eucharistic Mystery.[106]

The *Didache* gives extensive attention to reconciliation in Eucharistic meetings:

> And on the day of the Lord assemble yourselves together and break bread; and give thanks after having confessed also your transgressions, that your sacrifice may be pure. And let not any man that is at variance with his fellow come together with you until they be reconciled, that your sacrifice be not polluted.[107]

The *Syriac Didascalia* commands the bishop to convene reconciliation meetings on the second day of the week (Monday),

> That there be opportunity for you until the Sabbath, that ye may arrange the matter, and make peace, and pacify them on the Sunday.

It also adds,

> Therefore when you sit to judge, let the two individuals come and stand together; we do not call them brethren until there be peace between them.[108]

---

[104] Romans 16.6; 1 Corinthians 16.20; 2 Corinthians 13.12
[105] 1 Corinthians 10.17.
[106] Dix, *op. cit.*, 107-108.
[107] Allen, *op. cit.*, 9, Didache 14.1-2
[108] Allen, *op. cit.*, 61.

Since the second century, and thereafter, the liturgical kiss reached its prominence as a Christian symbol, an immediate prelude to the Eucharist. It was a symbol of "*the unity of the Spirit in the bond of peace.*"[109]

The holy kiss was found clearly in the Greek text of the Epistle to the Romans: "*Greet one another with a holy kiss*" (Ἀσπάσαθτε αλλήλους ἐν φιλήματι ἁγίῳ).[110] Justin the Martyr also mentions the holy kiss clearly in his First Apology referring to it as the preparation for the Eucharist, and a conclusion to the prayers that precede the sanctification of the mysteries.

The holy kiss is the entry into the anaphora. As for all the prayers before the holy kiss, they are called in the West the *Ordinary Mass*, which are customary or familiar prayers repeated in every liturgy. The prayers after the holy kiss are determined by the type of liturgy we are praying, whether it be that of Basil of Caesarea, Gregory the Theologian, or Cyril of Alexandria in the Coptic rite, or by other liturgies.

Gregory Dix explains that in the third century the deacon cries out while standing beside the bishop's seat, while the congregation exchanges the holy kiss, saying: "Is there anyone who is keeping any grudge against his fellow?" It is as a final warning before the bishop makes peace between the congregation members. This warning

---

[109] Ephesians 4.3
[110] Romans 16.16

by the deacon, modified extensively, became an elongated response.[111]

The kiss of peace precedes the anaphora to apply the instructions of the Gospel:

> Therefore, if you bring your gift to the altar, and there remember that your brother has something against you, leave your gift there before the altar, and go your way. First be reconciled to your brother, and then come and offer your gift.[112]

The *Apostolic Constitutions* teaches, commenting on these words of the Lord,

> ... because the gifts of God are the prayer and thanks of each person. If there is fault between you and you brother, or to your brother over you, then your prayers will not be heard before God, nor will your thanks be accepted, because of the anger between you and your brother.

This biblical instruction caused all the ancient liturgical rites, East and West, to integrate the holy kiss before offering the oblations. We find this tradition clearly in the *Apostolic Constitutions*. John Chrysostom (347-407) mentioned that this was practiced during his days.[113] The kiss of peace in the Greek liturgies known as the *Greek Liturgy of Mark* and the *Greek Liturgy of James* comes before the final prayers of the offertory.[114]

---

[111] Dix, *op. cit.*, 106-107.
[112] Matthew 5.23-24
[113] *PG*, 61, c527.
[114] Baumstark, Anton. *Comparative Liturgy*, English Edition (F.L. Cross, London, 1958), 136.

The sanctification of the mysteries begins and is completed on the basis of love. The Eucharist is dangerous without love, becoming a dreadful judgment, punishment, and death, instead of forgiveness and eternal life.[115]

The Eucharist is Christ's love poured out in us. If we cannot love each other, we should not dare approach the Holy Mysteries. It is the mystery of thanksgiving established on love. Through it, the Father dwells in our hearts to reconcile us with the Holy Spirit so that through it we become members with the saints in the household of God.

Theodore says:

> Through this kiss they create a type of unity and love between them. It is unfit for those who represent one body in the church, for one of them to hate his brother in the faith.[116]

The Kiss of Peace in the Various Rites

All the rites know the call of the deacon: "Greet one another with a holy kiss," as mentioned in Romans 16.16; however, the call differs slightly in its interpretation based on the local language of each church. In some churches, the deacons say, "Greet one to the other with a holy kiss," or, "Let us greet each to the other with a holy kiss."

---

[115] 1 Corinthians 11.27-30
[116] *Catec. Hom.*, 15.40.

The Church of Constantinople was unique in saying, "Let us love one another" (ἀγαπησωμεν ἀλλήλους). Certainly, the deacon's call here, "Let us love," means, "Let us kiss," as is the case in the Syriac rendering.[117]

In his letter to Demetrius, John Chrysostom points to the deacon's call: "Let us kiss one another" (Ἀσπαζόμενοι ἀλλήλους). This call is found verbatim in the *Syriac Liturgy of James the Brother of the Lord*.[118]

The liturgical kiss, in its full meaning, is a kiss with the mouth, as mentioned by the canons of the apostles, and the *Apostolic Constitutions* (Disdiscalia). The canons state from the beginning that the men greet the men, and the women greet the women, and that the men do not greet the women, nor the women the men, and the priests and deacons greet each other.

In some Eastern rites, limited phrases accompanied the holy kiss. In the Byzantine rite, one says to the other, "Christ is among us," and the other responds, "Now, and He remains with us." As for the Coptic Church, it chants hymns during the holy kiss rite known as the ἀσπασμός in Greek, which means greeting.

Clement of Alexandria (150-215) criticized the ecclesiastic kiss. He says:

---

[117] The verb *to love* and *to kiss* are one in Syrian. The expression "love his hand," means, "kiss his hand," in some Egyptian cities in Upper Egypt, and in some cities in Mesopotamia in Syria.
[118] Ignatius Aphrem II, *op. cit.*, 163.

> There are others who have no other job but to make the sound of the kiss echo throughout the church, although it should be understood on a mystical level. The apostles call the kiss *holy*.[119]

His criticism did not halt or modify this tradition. Rather, it continued to be an essential part of the liturgy. We know from the writings of Justin the Martyr (100-165), Cyril of Jerusalem (315-386), John Chrysostom (347-407), and Augustine of Hippo (354-430) that the believers exchange the holy kiss, with a kiss.[120]

Cyril of Jerusalem says,

> Do not assume that this kiss is as that which friends are used to at meetings. It is not of this kind; this unites the souls, and clears away all envy... it is a sign of uniting the souls.[121]

Augustine of Hippo says,

> It is a sign of peace. What the lips show on the outside exists in the heart on the inside.

John Chrysostom says,

> When each one kisses the mouth of the other, we kiss the entry to the altar. Therefore, may none of us do this with a deceptive conscience... because the kiss is holy, as Paul says, 'Greet one another with a holy kiss.' (1 Corinthians 16.20)
> (Catechism teachings 11.34)

---

[119] Clement of Alexandria, *Paedagogus*, 3.11
[120] Ignatius Aphrem II, *op. cit.*, 242-243.
[121] Cyril of Jerusalem, *Catechetical Homily*, 23

In the *Syriac Didascalia (Didascalia Apostolorum)*, the deacon, at the moment of the kiss, calls out with a loud voice, "If anyone has anything against another…" He offers a final warning so that the bishop may reconcile disputes between anyone.

Placing the holy kiss before the anaphora is a shared characteristic of the Eastern rites (as opposed to the Western), except for the Byzantine rite in which the creed falls between the holy kiss and the anaphora. In the rite of the Church of Rome, the kiss of peace comes immediately before communion.[122] This unique Roman idiosyncrasy was transferred to the Milan rite. It is a strange feature, having no relation to the Western rites.[123] There is evidence to prove the presence of this practice in the Roman Church rite since 416.[124]

The holy kiss was confined, in some Eastern churches, to the clergy, inside the altar. However, this was not the case in the ancient origins of the kiss.

John Chrysostom says in one of his sermons:

> When the time comes to exchange the kiss, all used to greet all. The clergy kissed the bishop. The men kissed the men, and the women kissed the women.

---

[122] Dix, *op. cit.*, 108.
[123] This is what motivated some liturgical researchers to assume that the deacon's response in the Coptic rite, "Offer in order…" which follows, "Greet one another," refers to coming forward to partake of the holy communion from the holy mysteries.
[124] Dix, *op. cit.*, 501-502.

the other on the right side of the neck, and the other repays with a similar kiss to the neck.[128]

Ibn Kabar (d. 1324) mentions:

The men kiss the men, and the women kiss the women, and each bows to the other.[129]

Ibn Kabar (d. 1324) also mentions,

When the Aspasmos is read, the deacon says, Greet one another with a holy kiss (ⲁⲥⲡⲁⲍⲉⲥⲑⲉ ⲁⲗⲗⲏⲗⲟⲩⲥ ⲛ̄ ⲫⲓⲗⲓⲙⲁⲧⲓ ⲁ︎ⲅⲓⲟⲩ) so the men greet the men and the women greet the women, and each kneels to the other, and the cantors chant what is appropriate for the day... then the prospherein is lifted up as the lifting up of the stone which was rolled away from the door of the tomb, and our Lord removing His wrappings and linen cloths from His pure honorable body at the time of the resurrection.[130]

Pope Gabriāl V (1409-1427) writes:

Then they recite the litany of reconciliation in its entirety. When the deacon says ⲁⲣⲓⲁⲥⲡⲁⲍⲉⲥⲑⲉ the priests greet each other, and the deacons each other. This is symbolic of the reconciliation He made between the heavenlies and the earthlies. The apostle says that He came to reconcile between the heavenlies and the earthlies. Whoever is carrying something towards his brother, whether necessary or unnecessary, leaves it at this time, and greets him. His kiss to him cannot be deceit, corruption, or cunning, becoming as Judas who kissed his Master with

---

[128] Yoḥanna Ibn A'bī Zakaria Ibn Sebā', *op. cit.*, 217.
[129] Shams al-Ri'āsa Abū al-Barakāt, *The Lamp of Darkness and the Clarification of the Service (Miṣbāḥ al-ẓulma wa 'īdāḥ al-khidma)*, op. cit.,
[130] *Ibid.* This is the exposition known in our church for the meaning of prospherein.

deceit, corruption, or cunning. When they have greeted each other, and kissed each other with love and a pure intent, they share in fellowship with the angels in sanctification, that is, Holy, Holy, Holy, Lord of Hosts, heaven and earth are full of Your holy glory.[131]

<u>The Current Shape of the Holy Kiss in the Various Rites</u>

Currently, in the Coptic rite, the congregation greet each other with both hands, likewise the clergy of equal church rank with each other. In the Syriac rite, the deacon takes the hands of the priest between his hands, then wipes his face with his hands. In the Armenian rite, each one bows to his companion. In the Byzantine rite, when more than one priest serves in the liturgy, each greets the other, as the older says, "Christ is with us, in us, and by us," and the younger answers, "He was, is, and will be." If the bishop/patriarch is the one offering the holy sacrifice, they greet the oblations, then his hand, then each other, in succession. In the Church of Rome, this rite is unaccompanied by any prayers or chants.

---

[131] Pope Gabriāl V, *op. cit.*, 77. It is truly amazing that the *Trinitarian Mystery in Pastoral Care* by a church teacher from the middle ages mentions exactly what was mentioned here by Pope Gabriāl V, but with slight changes, which reveals that both their writings are retrieved from an even more ancient source. This book says, "The priest greets the priest, and the deacon the deacon, and the people like them greet each other. This is symbolic of the reconciliation the Lord made between the heavenlies and the earthlies, broke the old with the new. Whoever is carrying something towards his brother, leaves it at this time, and greets him. His kiss to him cannot be deceit as Judas who kissed his Master with deceit, corruption, or cunning. Then they share in fellowship with the angels in sanctification, that is, Holy, Holy, Holy, Lord of Hosts, heaven and earth are full of Your holy glory." (p. 22)

The Aspasmos Accompanying the Deacon's Response to the Holy Kiss

The Greek word ἀσπασμός (*Aspasmos*) means *welcome, greeting, kiss,* or *salutation*. The *kiss of peace* or the *holy kiss* is the traditional practice, after which immediately begins the Eucharistic Liturgy in all the East.

In the Coptic Church, there is the *Aspasmos Adam* and *Aspasmos Watos*; they are two tunes to two hymns chanted by the entire congregation in the Divine Liturgy.

Aspasmos Adam

The *Aspasmos Adam* is chanted after the deacon's response, "Greet one another with a holy kiss,"[132] in either the annual tune, or a tune specific to a church event. The deacon then continues his response after the conclusion of the *Aspasmos*, "Lord have mercy…"

Aspasmos Watos

The *Aspasmos Watos* is chanted immediately before the Cherubic Chant In the Coptic Liturgy, the standard *Aspasmos Watos* is "The cherubim worship

---

[132] What is mentioned in the *Book of the Deacon's Service* is not accurate where it says that that *Aspasmos Adam* is said before the deacon's response, "Greet one another," since necessarily comes afterwards. See the Euchologion (1902).

You, and the seraphim glorify You, proclaiming and saying,"[133] followed by the Cherubic chant.

Now, let us discuss the different *Aspasmos Adams* that accompany the deacon's response, "Greet one another."

Pope Gabriāl V did not mention anything about the *Aspasmos Adam*. He only referred to it as a chant:

> When they finish the chant at the time of reconciliation, the deacon says prospherein.[134]

Ibn Kabar (d. 1324) gives us specific details about the *Aspasmos Adam* during his time:

> When the Aspasmos is read, the deacon says, 'Greet one another with a holy kiss…' and the cantors chant what is appropriate for that day. For annual days they say, 'Ⲡⲭⲥ Ⲡⲉⲛⲛⲟⲩϯ' or they say, 'Greet with a kiss - ⲁⲣⲓ`ⲁⲥⲡⲁⲍⲉⲥⲑⲉ. On the Passover, Feasts, and Holy Fifty Days…[135] For Nativity, they say, 'Ⲣⲁϣⲓ ⲟⲩⲟϩ ⲑⲉⲗⲏⲗ.' Between Epiphany and Nativity they might say, 'Ⲛⲁϥⲛⲁⲩ ϧⲉⲛ ⲛⲓⲃⲁⲗ.' In limited times, they might not say that, but might suffice to say, 'Ϩⲓⲧⲉⲛ ⲛⲓⲉⲩⲭⲏ,' during the commemoration days of the martyrs, saints, and angels. The name of each one being mentioned on his day. They might suffice to say, 'Ⲧⲉⲛⲟⲩⲱϣⲧ.' And when they say it, they all bow down to

---

[133] H G Bishop Serapion, and H G Bishop Youssef., *op. cit.*, 185.
[134] Pope Gabriāl V, *op. cit.*, 77.
[135] I placed the ellipsis because I assume Ibn Kabar's manuscript is missing some Coptic words, since he did not mention the *Aspasmos* chanted during the Passover and Holy Fifty Days, unless the text means as follows: "or they say, 'Greet with a kiss' on the Passover, Feasts, and Holy Fifty Days, in which case the *Aspasmos* mentioned would be specific to the Passover.

God on days of worship, or they kneel on days when bowing down is not allowed. Most worship...[136]

From what precedes by Ibn Kabar we learn what follows:

- The regular annual *Aspasmos* during his time is: 'Ⲡⲭⲥ Ⲡⲉⲛⲛⲟⲩϯ' (O Christ our God). This is the same *Aspasmos* found in the Euchologion (1902), yet, its prelude is 'Ⲡⲭⲥ ⲡⲉⲛⲥⲱⲧⲏⲣ' that is 'O Christ our Savior':

    O Christ our Savior, make us worthy of Your holy peace in heaven. That we many praise You with the cherubim and the seraphim, proclaiming and saying: Holy, holy, holy, O Lord, the Pantocrator, heaven and earth are full of Your glory and Your honor. Through the intercessions of the Theotokos, Saint Mary, O Lord, grant us the forgiveness of our sins. Through the intercessions of the three holy luminaries Michael, Gabriel, and Raphael, O Lord, grant us the forgiveness of our sins. Through the intercessions of the four incorporeal beasts and the twenty-four presbyters, O Lord, grant us the forgiveness of our sins. Through the intercessions of the seven archangels, and all the heavenly orders, O Lord, grant us the forgiveness of our sins.

    The Euchologion continues:

    Then they address our fathers the apostles and whomever they choose from among the martyrs, saints, and patriarchs. Then they end with, "We worship You O Christ.

---

[136] Shams al-Riʾāsa Abū al-Barakāt, *The Lamp of Darkness and the Clarification of the Service (Miṣbāḥ al-ẓulma wa 'īḍāḥ al-khidma)*, op. cit.,

Based on this, the beloved reader can understand the origin of the response of "Through the intercessions of the Theotokos, Saint Mary." This response became standardized in our daily liturgies.

Why do we call it an abridged *Aspasmos Adam*?

Actually, the *Aspasmos Adam* was not a fixed response throughout the year for all occasions; it is an *Aspasmos* that can be chanted during the Fast and Feasts of the Virgin Mary, as any *Aspasmos Adam*. Even in this case, it was preceded by the fixed prelude, which did not vary with the changing feasts of the martyrs and saints, in the case of reciting this *Aspasmos*, which is: "O Christ our Savior, make us worthy of Your holy peace in heaven..." This is also only an annual *Aspasmos*.

Here, we need to realize the precise connection between the congregation's practice of exchanging the holy kiss and their prayer during this kiss, so that the Lord makes us worthy of His heavenly peace through the intercessions of the Theotokos, Virgin Mary.

When the response, "Through the intercessions of the Theotokos" was severed from the context of the previously mentioned *Aspasmos*, it severed the connection between the meaning of what we practice and what we say, i.e., seeking the intercessions of the Virgin at this specific moment? However, when we ask for the Lord to make us worthy of His heavenly peace through the intercessions of the Virgin, the angels, the apostles, the martyrs, or the saints, the congregation conclude this request by asking for the forgiveness of sins through these intercessions because it is the moment of the kiss of peace, reconciliation, forgiveness of sins, and pardoning of iniquities.

- From the words of Ibn Kabar, it also becomes clear to us that detaching the stanza specific to the Virgin, or other stanza, from the aforementioned *Aspasmos Adam*, happened during his days when there was a need for brevity, when it sufficed asking the intercessions or prayers during the commemorations of the Virgin Mary, the angels, the martyrs, and the saints.

- Ibn Kabar mentions that in the case of not chanting the *Aspasmos*, the response is limited to Ⲧⲉⲛⲟⲩⲱϣⲧ (We worship You O Christ). And when they say it, they all bow down to God on days of worship, or they kneel on days when bowing down is not allowed. And most kneel.

"We worship You O Christ...," which now comes in our responses immediately following the *Aspasmos Adam*, and immediately preceding another Greek response, "A mercy of peace, a sacrifice of praise,"[137] is a response that has no relationship with the *Aspasmos Adam* (since it can be said without it), nor with the Greek response following it, which initiates the *Liturgy of the Believers*. The latter response is chanted immediately after lifting up the prospherein off the oblations.

---

[137] H G Bishop Serapion, and H G Bishop Youssef., *op. cit.*, 179.

For this reason, Euchologion (1902) relies on the manuscripts in explaining that after the deacon's response: "Offer, in order. Stand with trembling. Look towards the East. Let us attend," the congregation answers, "A mercy of peace, a sacrifice of praise."

In the Vatican Manuscript No. 17 (Coptic/1288 CE) we read in the beginning of the *Liturgy of Basil*, addressed to the Father:

> The deacon says, 'Come forward people, stand up, look towards the East.' And the congregation say, 'Mercy, peace, and a full sacrifice.'

In the Oxford Manuscript No. 360 (Huntington), the response comes in Arabic:

> Mercy, peace, sacrifice, and praise.[138]

Despite the difference in the Arabic translations of the Greek response, all the manuscripts contain the Greek text of the response of "Ἔλεος εἰρήνης. Θυσία αἰνέσεως."[139]

In this regard, Ibn Sebāʿ says,

> When he reaches the point of lifting up the prospherein, he asks for the servants saying: 'Stand upright. Stand with reverence. Stand with request. Stand with fear of God. And

---

[138] The Monastery of Macarius Manuscripts No. 136 and 137 (Rites) mention, "Mercy, peace, and a rich sacrifice"; Manuscript No. 134 (Rites) mentions, "Mercy, peace, and a sweet offering."
[139] In the *Syriac Liturgy of James the Brother of the Lord*, and in the *Byzantine Liturgy of John Chrysostom*, the first word to this response is Ἔλεον.

answer.' And the people answer, 'Peace, mercy, and a sacrifice.'[140]

Lifting up the prospherein comes after the end of the *Aspasmos Adam* (if chanted), or after chanting, "We worship You O Christ..."

Ibn Kabar says that after the people chant, "We worship You O Christ..." and they all bow down to God or kneel,

> The prospherein is lifted up akin to lifting up the stone which was rolled from the door of the tomb, and our Lord removing His wrappings and linen cloths from His pure honorable body at the time of the resurrection.[141]

Thus, the rite explains to us the secret to our entry to heaven. The priest, with the deacon opposite him, lift up the prospherein, moving it up gently so the sound of the bells attached to it is heard, a symbol of the resurrection of our Lord, which is the secret to our preparation for heaven, its spiritual goods, which is the body of our Lord and precious blood; the tree of life which keeps those who eat of it from dying.

Root and Source of the Hymn of the Intercessions

Here, I must refer to what I have discussed in the chapter on the *Liturgical roots of the Offertory Rite*,[142]

---

[140] Yoḥanna Ibn A'bī Zakaria Ibn Sebā', *op. cit.*, 246-247.
[141] Shams al-Ri'āsa Abū al-Barakāt, *The Lamp of Darkness and the Clarification of the Service (Miṣbāḥ al-ẓulma wa 'īdāḥ al-khidma), op. cit.,*
[142] Please refer to the first volume of this series on the *Divine Liturgy: The Mystery of the Kingdom*

concerning the roots and sources of the hymn of the intercessions. This abovementioned *Aspasmos Adam*, with its accompanying intercessions or prayers specific to the Virgin, the angels, the martyrs, and the saints, is the root of the hymn of the intercessions, which we recite today before reading from the Epistles of Paul the Apostle. It was originally chanted at the response of the holy kiss. This *Aspasmos Adam* used to select one intercession in accordance with the feast of the martyr or saint of the day. Currently, and after this hymn has been moved to be before the reading of the Pauline epistle, it gradually grew until it became several stanzas, that are currently concluded with the stanza for the patriarch and the bishop. It was not so before. Concerning this, Ibn Kabar mentions:

> It might suffice to say, 'ϩⲓⲧⲉⲛ ⲛⲓⲉⲩⲭⲏ,' during the commemoration days of the martyrs, saints, and angels. The name of each one being mentioned on his day.

Hegumen ʿAbd al-Massīh Salīb al-Massʿūdī al-Baramūsī (1848-1935) added:

> ...Then they address our fathers the apostles and whomever they choose from among the martyrs, saints, and **patriarchs**.

I previously pointed[143] that the first indicator to this hymn in its current position was in the *Book of the Service of the Deacon* published in 1938.

---

[143] Please refer to the first volume of this series on the *Divine Liturgy: The Mystery of the Kingdom*.

- The other *Aspasmos* mentioned by Ibn Kabar is "ⲁⲣⲓⲁ☐ⲥⲡⲁⲍⲉⲥⲑⲉ - greet." Its words are:

    Greet with a holy kiss, purify your hearts from all evil. Be ready for the gift of God, until you partake of these mysteries. Thus, we will gain mercy and forgiveness of our sins, according to His great mercy. We worship You O Christ…

Notice the uniqueness of this *Aspasmos* and the depth of its words. However, why did it fall into oblivion despite the intricacy of the meanings that agree with the moment of the holy kiss? Will someone who is zealous for his church restore this hymn with its unique meaning?

- Ibn Kabar also mentions that the *Aspasmos Adam*, 'Ⲣⲁϣⲓ ⲟⲩⲟϩ ⲑⲉⲗⲏⲗ,' is chanted on the Nativity Feast. This *Aspasmos* is retrieved from the first and second stanzas of the fifth section of the Monday Theotokia:

    Rejoice and be happy, O human race, for God so revealed His love to the world, that He gave His beloved Son for those who believe in Him, so that they may live forever.

- Ibn Kabar also mentions that the *Aspasmos Adam*, 'Ⲛⲁϥⲛⲁⲩ ϧⲉⲛ ⲛⲓⲃⲁⲗ,' is chanted between the Nativity and Epiphany Feasts. This *Aspasmos* is retrieved from the first stanza of the fourth section of the Monday Theotokia:

    Isaiah has seen the mysteries of Emmanuel with prophetic insight. Wherefore the great prophet shouted out proclaiming and saying, 'For unto us a child is born, unto us a son is given, the government shall be upon his shoulder...'

It is worth mentioning that the current *Aspasmos Adam* chanted on the Nativity Feast are the third and fourth stanzas of this same fourth section of the Monday Theotokia. As for Ibn Kabar, he added the first two stanzas of this section.

There are a plethora of *Aspasmos Adams*, especially ones pertaining to the Lordly feasts, that became integrated into the Coptic Liturgy since the beginning of the twentieth century. Hegumen ʿAbd al-Massīh Salīb al-Massʿūdī al-Baramūsī included many of these *Aspasmos Adams* in his Euchologion from some manuscripts at the Monastery of Virgin Mary (El-Baramous), after undergoing some linguistic corrections.[144]

Meaning of the Deacon's response: "Offer in order"

In the response of "Greet one another with a holy kiss," the deacon subsequently says, "Offer in order, Stand with trembling. Look towards the East. Let us attend." This expression was translated into Arabic as "Come forward in order..." such that some translated this as a call to come forward for communion from the holy mysteries. Where did this ambiguity come from that confuses between offering the oblations and

---

[144] Many of the seasonal *Aspasmos Adam* or *Watos* are retrieved from the Theotokias or Doxologies. Sometime, the *Aspasmos* also acts as the Praxis response for this occasion, which is in turn one of the verses of the symbols.

partaking of the divine mysteries? This is what I will explain in the following lines.

The Greek word, προσφέρειν (prospherein), is what caused this confusion in the Arabic translation. προσφέρειν (prospherein) stems from the verb προσφέρω (prosphero), which is mentioned forty-eight times in the New Testament. It was translated forty-seven times as "to offer – to present – to set before one – to bring one thing near another," and once as "to deal with."[145]

The literal translation to of this response in Greek is, "Offer in order, Stand with trembling. Look towards the East. Let us attend."[146] The precise translation to this Greek response is, "Stand with trembling to offer according to custom..." that is, to offer your oblations according to habit. The translation could also be, "offer according to custom, stand with trembling..."

Hence, it is clear that this response is not a call to come forward for communion from the holy mysteries, but to offer the oblations according to the custom or

---

[145] Hebrews 12.7
[146] This is according to the *Liturgy of Cyril*, but in the *Liturgies of Basil and Gregory*, this response is preceded by the deacon saying: "Lord have mercy. Lord have mercy. Lord have mercy. Yea, Lord, who are Jesus Christ, the Son of God, hear us and have mercy upon us" (a Coptic response). In the *Coptic Liturgy of Gregory*, it is further extended by: "Let us stand well, let us stand reverently, let us stand earnestly, let us stand in peace, let us stand in the fear of God, with trembling and contrition" (a Greek response). This last response is found verbatim in the Byzantine Church Liturgies, and in the *Apostolic Constitutions*.

habit for the divine liturgy to begin. Thus, the rite of offering the lamb did not precede the *Liturgy of the Word* as is the case today, but followed it, since the catechumens were not allowed to participate in the prayers. They were only allowed to listen to the epistles, the Holy Gospel, the sermon, and some directions that were concluded with the *Litany of the Catechumens*.

The timing of this response is distinct in that the time to offer the oblations immediately follows the call for the holy kiss. This is the ancient rite that prevailed in the universal church, not only in the Coptic Church.

What also supports this point is that this response in the Greek Church until this day is: "Let us stand well, let us stand with fear, let us attend, let us offer the holy oblation with peace," to which the congregation respond, "Peace mercy, sacrifice of praise." Here it is clear that that deacon's call is for offering the oblations after concluding the *Liturgy of the Word*,[147] or more precisely, following the holy kiss.

Justin the Martyr (100-165) is the first author who states that the kiss is a prerequisite to the offertory.[148]

In the *Apostolic Tradition* [4:1-3] of Hippolytus of Rome, the offertory is immediately after the holy kiss:

> When the bishop breaks, let him give each one, the kiss of peace, kissing him, because he has become worthy of this. Let the deacons bring to him the offerings, and he places his hand, with all the priests on the offerings, and thanks

---

[147] Cf. Brightman, *op. cit.*, 309 ff.
[148] Dix, *op. cit.*, 108.

> saying, 'The Lord be with you all.' The people reply, 'And with your spirit.' The bishop says, 'Lift up your hearts.' The people reply, 'We lift them up onto the Lord.' The bishop says, 'Let us give thanks unto the Lord,' the people reply, 'It is meet and right to do so.'[149]

Here it becomes clear to us that the holy kiss has become one of the established standards in the liturgical rite, since it must come at this exact ritual point, that is, immediately before offering the oblations, as in the Eucharistic rite before Nicaea, in all places East and West.[150]

In the *Coptic Apostolic Canons*, offering the oblations follows the holy kiss and the *Liturgy of the Word*.

> When they conclude the prayer, they greet each other with a kiss. The deacons enter with the offering to the bishop (the offertory), and the bishop thanks over the bread and chalice, to become Christ's body and blood which was shed for all of us, who believed in Him.
> (Canon 1.34)

The *Coptic Apostolic Canon* [1.52] elucidates this point with all clarity when mentioning that after the deacon says, "Let us stand in fear and trembling," he says, "prospherein." Then the canon says, "When this is done, let the deacon come with the bread to the bishop at the altar…" Thus, it is clear that the offertory is after the deacon says, "prospherein."

---

[149] Warren, *op. cit.*, 108.
[150] Dix, *op. cit.*, 108.

But why was this part of the liturgy rearranged, specifically this deacon's response and the word *prospherein*? In fact, some rite expositors considered it to mean "come forward," that is, come forward to partake of the oblations, and not, offer the oblation?

This confusion occurred because of the overlap in this part of the liturgy between the Eastern and Western rites. The Eastern rite (which preserved antiquity) preserved the rite of the offertory following the holy kiss. The Western rite, especially the Church of Rome, moved the holy kiss to the end of the Divine Liturgy, to be immediately following communion. This caused the confusion between the Eastern and Western rites.

Gregory Dix comments:

> What we need to know is that the Roman texts do not point to the holy kiss in the Roman Church rite "for two hundred years after Hippolytus [of Rome];[151] and that then we find its position has shifted in the local Roman rite [only] from before the offertory to before the communion." This differs from all early Christian rites East and West.[152]

The Church of Rome retrieved the rite of the holy kiss before the communion (instead of the offertory) from the churches of North Africa[153] towards the end of the fourth century.[154] The Lord's Prayer was recited between the Fraction and communion in the churches of North Africa. This practice was retrieved from an

---

[151] In the first third of the third century.
[152] Dix, *op. cit.*, 108.
[153] Augustine, ep. Lix.
[154] Dix, *op. cit.*, 108.

ancient ritual in the Church of Jerusalem, where the holy kiss comes immediately after "Forgive us our trespasses as we forgive those who trespass against us" in the Lord's Prayer.[155]

We do not find this rite in the Church of Rome during that time, since the Lord's Prayer is not found in the Eucharistic Liturgy before the time of Pope Gregory the Great (d. 604).[156]

When Rome adopted the Lord's Prayer into the Eucharistic Liturgy, like the rest of Christendom, she inserted it, not after the Fraction (like the churches of North Africa), but between the Eucharistic Prayer and the Fraction, as in the rite of the Church of Jerusalem. The Lord's Prayer comes in the Church of Rome before the Fraction. Thus, the holy kiss parted from the phrase, "forgive us our trespasses...," in the Lord's Prayer, as is the case with the churches of North Africa in the fourth century.[157]

Gregory Dix informs us that the Church of Rome adopted the new ritual place for the holy kiss,

> not very long before 416, when the matter is brought to our knowledge by a letter from Pope Innocent I to his neighbor, Bishop Decentius of Gubbio, urging that other Italian churches near Rome (which still retained the kiss in its

---

[155] *Ibid.*

[156] *Ibid.*

[157] *Ibid.* The North Africa rite: Eucharistic Prayer – Fraction – Lord's Prayer – kiss – Communion. The Roman Church rite: Eucharistic Prayer – Lord's Prayer – Fraction –kiss – Communion.

original position before the offertory) ought to conform to current Roman practice on this and other points.[158]

Other Western churches adopted the order of the Church of Rome, and of the churches of North Africa, in moving the holy kiss to be immediately before communion, as in the Celtic rite in England.[159]

The Church of Rome was not alone in changing the ritual position of the holy kiss; rather, Eastern Christendom predated Rome in this change by moving the kiss to be after the offertory rather than before it. This change first occurred in Jerusalem in 348. In Antioch, it remained in its original place during the time of John Chrysostom (347-407) when the practice of the Church of Jerusalem began to spread during his time in the Church of Syria. In the fifty century, the kiss settled into its new place after the offertory in the Church of Antioch, as in the Church of Jerusalem.[160]

This is also what happened in the churches of Mesopotamia, the Churches of Asia Minor, as their bishop Theodore (410) explains.[161]

During the fifth and sixth centuries, the Church of Constantinople adopted the habit of the Church of Jerusalem. From there it spread to all the Eastern churches.[162] The Church of Egypt remained alone up

---

[158] Dix, *op. cit.*, 109.
[159] *Ibid.*, 110.
[160] *Ibid.*, 109.
[161] *Ibid.*; Theodore, Cateicheses, V. (ed. Mingana, p. 92).
[162] This rite of Constantinople spread to the West also, where the Mozarabic rite in Spain adopted the Byzantine rite concerning the

until that time (the sixth century or thereafter) maintaining the kiss in its ancient ritual place before the offertory.[163]

The Church of Alexandria was the last church in the East to change the ritual ancient place of the kiss, to be after the offertory, and not before. Nevertheless, the deacon's response in the Coptic Church continued to preserve the ancient ritual order of this part of the Divine Liturgy: the call for the holy kiss is immediately followed by the call to offer the gifts.[164]

---

holy kiss along with some other Byzantine rites, perhaps in the sixth century, as a result of Justinian's occupation of Spain. Dix, *op. cit.*, 109.

[163] Dix, *op. cit.*, 109.

[164] This is replicated in the Church of Milan in the West. This Church followed the Roman Church in moving the holy kiss to the end of the liturgy, before communion, and yet the deacon in the Church of Milan, until this day, continues to announce the holy kiss in its ancient ritual position before the offertory. Dix, *op. cit.*, 109-110.

PRO-ANAPHORAL SECTION: THE GREATER THANKSGIVING PRAYER

Introduction

If the church services consisted only of the *Liturgy of the Word*, the church would not have been persecuted. The persecution the church was primarily because the church persisted in offering Eucharistic prayers in total secrecy, while the government had absolutely forbidden secret societies and communities. It was not possible for the church to make the Eucharistic prayers or the liturgy, public. These prayers are reserved for the members of the body of Christ, the community of believers. As such, before Nicaea, the liturgies were held in houses. More specifically, the liturgy was conducted in a large house of a wealthy member because in such a house total privacy was possible.[165]

Canon No. 260 of Gallienus granted Christians the freedom to meet. Although this law did not prevent some persecuting the Christians, it allowed the church a relative respite for about forty years, before the outrageous persecution by Emperor Diocletian.[166]

During this time, community meetings were held safely and special buildings were erected for Christian

---

[165] Dix, *op. cit.*, 24.
[166] *Ibid.*, 306.

worship as we can infer from the condition of the Church in Cirta (a small city in North Africa, now called Constantine in Algeria) where this church obtained its fancy furnishings: two gold chalices, six silver patents, seven silver lamps, and many other items.[167]

Meaning of Anaphora

Anaphora in Greek has many meanings. The most prominent definitions are: "carrying back" or "resorting to." In liturgical terminology, anaphora literally means "offering or lifting up the oblations." The word is made up of two syllables: *ana* which means *up*, and *phora* which means *lift, offer,* or *dress*. As such, Anaphora here means *lifting up the offering or oblation*. This term was applied to the main part of the Eucharistic prayers, the part that contains the sanctification, commemoration, and communion. The term covers most of the liturgical prayers; therefore, it was applied to the entire Eucharistic offering.

Anaphora for Syrians and Maronites is equivalent to *Qudas* (liturgy) for Copts. For the Assyrians it is labelled *Qadasho*.

It is intriguing that *Anaphora* is not the popular term in the Coptic Church, instead *Qudas*. Nevertheless, the Coptic title to any Coptic Liturgy in our Coptic manuscripts, and in the printed Euchologion is *Anaphora*.

---

[167] Dix, *op. cit.*, 24.

The title of the *Coptic Liturgy of Basil* is: ϯ ἀναφορα ν☐τε πια☐γιος Βασιλιος ε☐ φ☐ιωτ – The Anaphora of Basil of Caesarea to the Father.

The title of the *Coptic Liturgy of Gregory* is: ϯ ἀναφορα ν☐τε πια☐γιος Γρηγοριος πιθεολογος – The Anaphora of Gregory the Theologian.

The title of the *Coptic Liturgy of Mark* is: Ταρχη ν☐ϯα☐ναφορα ν☐τε πενιωτ ε☐θογαβ Μαρκος πια☐ποστολος θηε☐ταϥερβεβεον μ☐μος ν☐χε πιτ☐ρισμακαριος πια☐γιος Κυριλλος πιαρχηε☐πισκοπος. –The beginning of the Anaphora of our father Mark the Apostle, arranged by the thrice-blessed Cyril the head bishop (patriarch).

Pre-Anaphora Liturgical Dialogue

At the beginning of the *Liturgy of the Believers*, the liturgical dialogue commences between the priest and the congregation as follows:

> **Priest:** The Lord be with you all.
> **Congregation:** And with your spirit.
> **Priest:** Lift up your hearts.
> **Congregation:** We have them with the Lord.
> **Priest:** Let us give thanks to the Lord.
> **Congregation:** It is meet and right.[168]

This very ancient dialogue between the priest and the congregation is of great importance as the priest looks toward the West, facing the people, and engages

---

[168] H G Bishop Serapion, and H G Bishop Youssef., *op. cit.*, 183.

with them in a liturgical conversation. Afterwards, the priest turns back toward the East to begin praying, addressing God the Father with the exact words uttered by the congregation: "Meet and right."

We find that Ibn Sebā', from the thirteenth century, expounds on this liturgical dialogue:

> The priest turns his face to the West, and says, "The Lord be with you all," so the congregation answer him, "And with your spirit." Then the priest asks them, "Where are your hearts?" and they answer, "They are with the Lord." ...Then the priest tells them, "Thank the Lord," and they answer him, "meet, right, and just..."[169]

What is mentioned by Ibn Sebā' is confirmed by Vatican Manuscript No. 17 (Coptic) of 1288 CE. It mentions the following:

> The priest says, 'The Lord be with you all,' so the congregation say, 'And with your spirit.' The priest says, 'Where are your hearts?' The congregation say, 'They are with the Lord.' The priest says, 'Thank the Lord,' and the congregation say, 'worthy and deserving.'"

This is also what is mentioned in Oxford Manuscript No. 360 (Hunington).

We should note that there is no mention of any *signings*. As for Pope Gabriāl V, he was the first to mention the *signings* accompanying this dialogue, or perhaps he was explaining a ritual practice that was known before his time.

---

[169] Yoḥanna Ibn A'bī Zakaria Ibn Sebā', *op. cit.*, 247.

He writes:

> When the priest says, 'The Lord be with you all,' he signs the congregation as with a cross. When he says, 'Lift up your hearts,' he **looks towards the East** and signs the servants once. When he says, 'Let us give thanks to the Lord,' he signs himself once, and **returns to the East**, and says, 'worthy and just...'[170]

We cannot overlook his words that when the priest says, 'Lift up your hearts,' he looks towards the East. Pope Gabriāl V mentions a second time that he "returns to the East, and says, 'worthy and just.'" Here, the inconsistencies between the ritual practices he mentions are clear. However, they can be resolved only if Pope Gabriāl V means that the priest turns and faces the East after having faced the West while in conversation with the congregation in the third and final dialogue with the congregation.

The Euchologion (1902) mentions the second *signing* on the servants. In addition to what Pope Gabriāl V says, the Euchologion adds, "The priest says, as he signs the servants in the East, **to his right**, once." As if to say that the servants of the altar stand only to the right side of the altar, to the right of the priest. Despite this and that, the priest's words during this second *signing*, "lift up your hearts," is a call for all the people, not only to the servants.

The Euchologion (1902) includes marginal notes showing how to carry out these signings, which is not

---

[170] Pope Gabriel V, *Ritual Order, op. cit.*, 77.

mentioned by Pope Gabriāl V (1409-1427). The Euchologion states:

> The priest transfers to his left hand the cloth which he is holding,[171] and he takes in his right hand the cloth which is upon the oblation, and with it he makes the following three signs of the cross while keeping the two cloths in his hands[172] for the remainder of the liturgy, except the time of *signing* the oblations and the chalice, and the time of the fraction and thereafter...

These signings, accompanying this liturgical dialogue, were made through the offering cloths. In this regard, the manuscripts split into two: the first group (the majority) mentions the liturgical dialogue without mentioning any signings,[173] and the second group (the minority) mentions it accompanied by the signings[174] as is the case with Pope Gabriāl. Yet, no manuscripts mention the signings with the offering cloths, as was precisely mentioned by Euchologion (1902).

We need to understand the significance of placing the cloths on the hands, as explained by Pope Gabriāl V. His first mention of placing cloths on the priest's hands is after the conclusion of the litanies when the priest says, "Remember, O Lord, those who have

---

[171] This cloth has been placed over the prospherein in the shape of a triangle, a symbol of the tomb's seal. This is the one the priest lifts up before his eyes as he says, "According to Your good will, O God, fill our hearts with Your peace..."

[172] H G Bishop Serapion, and H G Bishop Youssef., *op. cit.*, 182.

[173] Such as the Library of the Monastery of Macarius Manuscripts No. 133, 134, 147 (Rites).

[174] Such as the Library of the Monastery of Macarius Manuscripts No. 136 (Rites).

brought unto You these gifts..." Pope Gabriāl V comments:

> When the deacon says, 'Let those who read,' the priest says the secret, 'Remember also, O Lord...'[175] After this, the priest takes upon his right hand a linen cloth. **From the time the priest handles the oblations with his hands, from the time he says, 'He took bread,' to the end of the liturgy, he cannot point with his hands to the people with unveiled hands, but wrapped in linen cloths out of respect and honor for what he touched.** When he finishes reading this secret, he wraps his right hand in a silk cloth, and points with it Westward towards the people, standing sideways, his left hand placed on the patent, asking Christ, reciting the blessing to its end.[176] Meanwhile, the deacon says, the commemoration for the reposed patriarchs, to its end...[177]

From what we have mentioned, we see that the rite according to Pope Gabriāl V means:

- The priest, before he says, "He took bread..." prayed with uncovered hands (this was repeated in several places in his book *Ritual Order*.)

- The signings accompanying the liturgical dialogue are done with uncovered hands.

---

[175] This is the beginning of the commemoration: "Remember also, O Lord, all those who have fallen asleep and reposed in the priesthood and in all the orders of the laity..." This is said inaudibly.

[176] I will explain this in detail when discussing the litanies and the commemoration.

[177] Pope Gabriāl V, *Ritual Order, op. cit.*, 82.

- Placing the cloth on the hands of the priest is only when the priest turns with them to point towards the people, this being in the later stages of the liturgy, after finishing the words of institution: "He took bread..."

- Only the right hand, the one with which the priest points towards the people, is to be covered with a silk cloth, while his left hand is to be unveiled and placed on the patent.

This rite was preserved in Euchologion (1902). What has been mentioned by Pope Gabriāl V was copied in the Euchologion, verbatim.

Bishop Boutros' Euchologion says,

> ... sign the people first, then the servants, and afterwards sign yourself last of all, remembering that you stand to serve the servants your companions and that it is not fitting for you to bypass another, even in the signings, although it is by your share. One who postpones himself receives calmness, peace, and humility.[178]

Overtime, there was a greater emphasis on the method of the signings instead of the liturgical dialogue, which took place between the priest and the congregation. From there, the ritual rubrics added that if the patriarch or the bishop are present, but is not serving, he is the one who signs the people, servants, and himself with the cross in silence,[179] while the

---

[178] Presbyter Samʿān Ibn Kalīl, *op. cit.*, 79.
[179] Notice that in this case the signings occur without the cloth.

celebrant priest says the words, without signing, except on himself. The same is repeated at *Holy, Holy, Holy*.

Origin of the Signings Accompanying the Liturgical Dialogue

These signings have an ancient Syriac origin, that was not integrated into the Coptic rite, except at a later date.

In the *Apostolic Constitutions* of Syriac origin, we read:

> The chief priest begins to pray inaudibly with the priests, donning splendid clothes and standing at the altar, and **makes the sign of the cross with his hand on his forehead, saying:** 'The grace of God the Pantocrator, the love of our Lord Jesus Christ, and the fellowship of the Holy Spirit, be with you all.' All answer him in one voice, 'And with your spirit.' The chief priest says, 'Lift up the heart,' the people, 'It is with the Lord. The chief priest, 'Let us thank the Lord,' the people, 'worthy and just.'
> (8.12.4,5)

From this it becomes clear that the signing accompanying the liturgical dialogue was done by the celebrant priest on his own forehead while saying the first part of the dialogue.

For the Syrians, the habit of signing moved to the bishop or celebrant priest signing the cross over the chest: beginning at the forehead and then moving to the left and then right shoulders. Afterwards, the priest signs the congregation in the same pattern.[180] Thus, the

---

[180] Ignatius Aphrem II, *op. cit.*, 246.

"And with your spirit," that is, "And with your spirit is also this peace."

Here, the significance of the congregation's participation in the liturgical prayers reveals its importance. The entire congregation are gathered together around the holy altar. They can address the priest, giving him the peace, and asking for the Lord's presence with him. This intimate relationship between the priest and the congregation is what prepares the entire church to rise to heaven. Here we do not forget the important liturgical request:

> Their prayers which they offer on our behalf and on behalf of all Your people, as well as ours on their behalf, receive them upon Your holy, heavenly, and rational altar...[185]

In the Church of Rome, as in the church of Milan, this liturgical greeting is in a simple form: "The Lord with you" (Dominus vobiscum). This form has a Greek origin in the Apostolic Constitutions of Hippolytus: "The Lord with you" (Ὁ Κύριος μεθ' ὑμῶν). We read in the *Apostolic Constitutions*:

> The bishop signs each of them on the forehead with the sign of the cross, and gives to each the kiss of peace, this mutual salvation passing. The Lord be with you (Ὁ Κύριος μεθ' ὑμῶν). And with thy spirit.[186]

In the Second Form, this liturgical greeting comes in a form specific to the Holy Trinity; nevertheless, it begins with the Person of the Son, the

---

[185] H G Bishop Serapion, and H G Bishop Youssef., *op. cit.*, 361.
[186] Warren, *op. cit.*, 89.

Name of Christ, expanding on the words in the Epistle to the Corinthians:

> The grace of the Lord Jesus Christ, and the love of God, and the communion of the Holy Spirit be with you all.[187]

This form was adopted by the Byzantine rite (with a slight adjustment):

> The grace of the Lord Jesus Christ, and the love of God the Father, and the communion of the Holy Spirit be with you all.

It spread there immensely, although its origin was not in Constantinople, but in Antioch, where John Chrysostom (347-407) used it in his sermons.[188]

The Third Form mentions the three Persons, but it begins with the Person of God the Father.

The response comes in this form in the *Liturgy of James the Brother of the Lord* (Syrian rite), whether in Greek or Syrian:

> The love of God the Father, and the grace of the only-begotten Son, and the fellowship and descent of the Holy Ghost be with you all, my brethren, evermore.[189]

Andre Tarby published this form according to the ancient Syriac rite:

---

[187] 2 Corinthians 13.14
[188] *PG*, 50, c.458.
[189] Brightman, *op. cit.*, 85.

> The love of God the Father, and the grace of our Lord and God and Savior Jesus Christ, and the communion of the Holy Spirit be with you all.[190]

This form originated in Jerusalem. In Book VIII of the *Apostolic Constitutions* gives us a somewhat embellished and expanded version, with some slight additions; the Armenian has a similar form.

This ancient ritual greeting was not said during the Eucharistic prayer only but was the bishop's greeting at any *agape* feast he attended with the congregation. The *Apostolic Tradition*, which was scribed before 235, explains this awesome ritual in the event of holding an evening dinner:

> When the evening comes, the bishop is there, and let the deacon bring the lantern. The bishop stands amid the believers, and before he blesses, he says, 'The Lord be with you,' and the people also say, 'And with your spirit." The bishop says, 'Let us give thanks to the Lord,' and the people say, 'He is worthy and due majesty and exaltation with glory.' And he does not say, 'Lift up your hearts' because it is said with the oblations.
> (26.16-21)

In all the liturgies, the response is "and with your spirit."

Lift up your hearts

This second part of the dialogue comes in three forms; no form is an abbreviation of another. This part

---

[190] Tarby, Andre. *La preire eucharistique de l'Eglise de Jerusalem*, 1972, 25-70.

is specific to the Eucharistic prayer, and the *Liturgy of Laqan*. It is not said at any other liturgical gathering. The three forms are as follows:

The First Form is:

[Lift up[191]] the hearts above (Ἄνω τὰς καρδίας).

This is the form that appeared in the Church of Jerusalem as we learn from the sermons of Cyril of Jerusalem (315-387) to the Catechumens.[192] Anastasius of Sinai also mentioned it.[193] Yet, this liturgical call most likely originated in the Church of Alexandria.

In the Armenian liturgy, these words are recited by the deacon instead of the priest:

Lift up in fear your hearts to the Lord.

In **the Second Form**, the priest says,

Lift up your mind (Ἄνω τὸν νοῦν).

This is an Antiochian rite, found in Book VIII of the *Apostolic Constitutions*.[194]

The Eastern Syrians, the Assyrians, use this expression in the liturgy of Addai and Mari.[195]

---

[191] *Lift up* is necessary here to translate this Greek expression, because τὰς καρδίας (hearts) comes as the direct object, and there is no clear verb in the sentence.
[192] *PG*, 33, c.1112.
[193] *PG*, 89, c.837A.
[194] Warren, *op. cit.*, 290.
[195] Brightman, *op. cit.*, 283.

In the ninth article by John Chrysostom on repentance, he cites the deacon's call to the believers saying, "Let us lift up our minds and hearts" (Ἄνω σχῶμεν ἡμων τὸν νοῦν καὶ τὰς καρδίας).

This call is only known in the *Syriac Liturgy of James the Brother of the Lord*.[196] As for the rest of the liturgies, the call is to lift up the hearts, not the minds.[197]

The Third Form comes as "The ears for the Lord," (Aures ad Dominum). This call is used in the ancient Spanish rite (Mozarabic rite). Yet, this last call deviated from all church rites, because, in ancient Christian patristic theology, and likewise in Pharaonic ethics, the heart is the seat of understanding and knowledge, and from it springs wisdom.

This primitive call developed into, "Let us hold up the hearts" (Ἄνω σχῶμεν τὰς καρδίας). This form was found in the Oxford F. Kacmarcik Codex, which contains the Greek text of the *Liturgy of Mark*, according to the Coptic rite.

The difference between the first and the third form is that the former ("the hearts above") might mean lifting the hearts up at this very moment only; however, the latter ("Let us hold up the hearts") means lifting them up and keeping them above always.

---

[196] *Ibid.*, 85.
[197] Ignatius Aphrem II, *op. cit.*, 195.

The third form later developed into, "Let us hold our hearts lifted up" (Ἄνω σχῶμεν τὰς καρδίας ἡμων), adding the pronoun ἡμων to include all those addressed. This form entered the Antiochian rite.

In Egypt, two forms were existent: the first is, "Let us lift up our hearts" (Ἄνω ἡμων τὰς καρδίας), and the second is, "Lift up your hearts" (Ἄνω ὑμων τὰς καρδίας). This second form is the one that prevailed in the Egyptian church.

These two forms are truly an extension of the first form, "The hearts above," which might be the original form that originated in Alexandria. This form is found in the *Apostolic Tradition* of Hippolytus, as we also see it in the rite of the Church of Rome and the Church of Milan. Here also, the Church of Rome retrieved from the Church of Alexandria the pro-anaphoral portion. Here, we are at a point of juncture between Alexandria and Rome, and also Jerusalem the bedrock of the Christian Church.[198]

Augustine of Hippo (354-430) says,

> The call 'Lift up your hearts,' is a general call in all world churches, East and West.

The congregation answers in all liturgies, "They are with the Lord," except the Eastern Syrians who answer, "Unto Thee, O God of Abraham, and of Isaac, and of Israel, O glorious king."[199]

---

[198] Baumstark, *op. cit.*, 84.
[199] Brightman, *op. cit.*, 283; A similar response may be found in the prayer of King Manasseh.

Beginning the Divine Liturgy means we begin to rise to heaven, to the sacrifice of the only-begotten Son, standing amid God's throne.[200] For, if we stand in your holy sanctuary O Lord, we are considered standing in heaven. When the congregation answer, "They are with the Lord," this means that we have entirely become with the Lord. Whoever receives the grace of lifting up his heart in this specific instant is one who is accustomed to direct his life towards heaven.

<u>*Let us give thanks to the Lord*</u>

This is the beginning of the greater thanksgiving prayer. This rite is known as the major Thanksgiving Prayer, or Thanksgiving Mystery. This liturgical text was recited in the Hebrew rite at the end of the meal over the cup of blessing, lifted up in the hand of the master of the feast. It was not fitting for it to be recited except if those attending were not less than one hundred people. It is a community call for a thanksgiving prayer. From here, it is the ancient form used by the synagogue.[201]

If those attending were about ten people, the minor thanksgiving prayer is recited, to which there is no response.[202]

---

[200] Revelation 5.6
[201] Dix, *op. cit.*, 79-80.
[202] Like the thanksgiving prayer said over the chalice in the offertory: "Let us give thanks…," which does not have an express response.

The Jewish thanksgiving prayer, which exactly matches the Christian thanksgiving prayer, is preceded by an invitation. In the Liturgy of Rome, this invitation is, "Let us thank the Lord our God," which is a literal translation of the command in the *Mishna* when at least one hundred persons gather to celebrate any regular Jewish meal.[203] Naturally, several additions were made to the old prayer that was recited at any regular Jewish meal since this ancient prayer became the sanctified prayer for the Sacramental Meal, the Sacred Sacrifice (the Eucharist), which we find in the *Didache*. We also should refer to the ancient Anaphora found in the *Apostolic Tradition* of Hippolytus. This ritual form, is the primary form for the major Thanksgiving Prayer, the form from which all Eucharistic forms were derived.[204]

Augustine of Hippo (354-430) says,

Let us thank Him, because, if He did not grant us his grace, our hearts would have remained clinging to earth. You witness to this and say, 'It right and just for us to thank Him who lifted up our hearts, to where our head is.'

All liturgies agree to this form, "Let us thank the Lord," except the Assyrian liturgy of Addai and Mari, where the priest says, "The offering is being offered unto God the Lord of all."[205]

Meet and Right

---

[203] Dix, *op. cit.*, 79, 127.
[204] Baumstark, *op. cit.*, 47.
[205] Brightman, *op. cit.*, 283.

This response, "Worthy and deserving," as in the older more precise Arabic translation, or "meet and right," a translation that appeared in the Middle Ages, is a very old response, known throughout the Christian world, East and West without exception. However, this response has no Jewish prototype. It's roots and origins stem from the Hellenic Greek world and became known in the early Christian language in its inception.[206]

Some err in understanding the meaning of this response, especially after its popular translation has become, "worthy and just," attributing to God the worthiness and justness. This would be true only if the response in Greek were in the masculine singular subject as Ἄξιος καὶ δίκαιος; however, the response appears in all the liturgies in the neutral singular as Ἄξιον καὶ δίκαιον.

Therefore, the response is not addressed to God, but urges us to offer thanksgiving; hence, "it is our duty and befitting for us to thank You," or, "it is meet and right for us to thank God."

Understanding the response comes easily from the context of the dialogue between the priest and the congregation: "It is meet and right to thank Him." This is the meaning of the response in Greek.

When the priest begins his prayer using the words of the congregation, redirecting them to God, he addresses God saying, "Meet and right..." He says, "It

---

[206] Baumstark, *op. cit.*, 82.

is fitting and becoming," or, "fitting and necessary,"[207] that is, "It is our duty and necessity to praise You, bless You, serve You, worship You, glorify You..." The words of the response, which the priest extracted from the congregation's mouth, begins with them the Eucharistic prayer. Otherwise, if the words, "worthy and just" had come as two adjectives specific to God, then the meaning would not have flowed in the priest's prayer.[208]

Here the priest places the cloth on his hands during this prayer. We read in Bishop Boutros's Euchologion,

> The reason for placing the cloths on the hands during prayer after reconciliation is that the priest hides his hands, declaring that the pure life-giving hands are the hands of our Lord Jesus Christ. And that His divine grace serves now. The one giving the grace is the only-begotten Son, the true high priest, to whom alone belongs the priesthood. Thus, the saying of the apostle is fulfilled: 'that we, without qualification, serve this better covenant.'[209]

Elements of the Major Thanksgiving Prayer

The *Major Thanksgiving Prayer* is the pro-anaphoral section. In the Greek text of the *Liturgy of Basil*, it is called Ἀρχὴ τῆς προσκομιδῆς, that is, "the beginning of the offertory." This is the prayer the priest says that immediately precedes the Cherubic praise.

---

[207] As in the Arabic translation of the Oxford F. Kacmarcik Codex.
[208] The cause of this misunderstanding is grammatical difficulty in the Arabic language.
[209] Presbyter Samʿān Ibn Kalīl, *op. cit.*, 74.

This *Major Thanksgiving Prayer* contains four main elements that form the entire eucharistic prayer, considering that it is a Eucharistic thanksgiving offered to God the Father through His Son Jesus Christ. Based on the words of Justin the Martyr (100-165), the eucharistic prayers from beginning to end is addressed to God the Father. All liturgies agree on this point, except the *Liturgy of Gregory* in the Coptic rite, as it addresses God the Son equally in its Greek and Coptic texts.

As for the East Syriac liturgy attributed to Addai and Mari, some of the prayers therein address the Trinity and some address the Son.[210]

The liturgical elements contained in the Eucharistic prayer of the *Major Thanksgiving Prayer* are mainly thanking God the Father for His work in creation, the incarnation of His only-begotten Son, the Passion of the Son, and the narration of Covenant Thursday (which always comes after the narration of the Passion).

We find this order in all the ancient liturgies, except for the *Liturgy of Serapion* which does not follow this order. As for the *Liturgy of Hippolytus* in the *Apostolic Tradition*, which is the oldest liturgical text to reach us, it followed this order in its abbreviated simplified form.

Concerning the first element, the Creation, it says,

---

[210] Brightman, *op. cit.*, 283-284.

> We offer to You thanks O God, through Your beloved Son Jesus Christ, Whom You send to us at the end of times, Savior and Redeemer, and messenger of Your will, Who is Your Word inseparable from You, through Whom You created all things.
> (4.4-5)

Concerning the second element, the *Liturgy of Hippolytus* says,

> Through Your goodwill you sent him from heaven to the womb of the Virgin, incarnate, who was carried in her, and was declared your Son born of the Holy Spirit and the Virgin.
> (4.6)

Concerning the third element, it says,

> Who fulfilled your will, and restored to you a holy people, extending his hands to the Passion, he saved those who believed in You from the pain. Who gave up himself to pain willfully, to kill death, and demolish the bonds of Satan, and step on Hades leading the righteous to the light, establishing order and revealing the resurrection.
> (4.7-8)

Concerning the fourth element, it says,

> He took bread and thanked you saying, 'take eat, this is my body, which is broken for you, for the forgiveness of sins. And also the cup, saying, this is my blood shed for you.
> (9.4)

The *Apostolic Constitutions* comments on this thanksgiving prayer saying,

> The bishop blesses, as we have already said. It is not necessary that he uses the exact words, exerting himself to say it by heart, offering thanks to God, but each person

the congregation except by, "Amen." This is what Justin the Martyr (100-165) mentions in his writing.[212]

Pro-Anaphoral Portion in the Liturgy of Serapion

According to Gregory Dix, we do not have an attested manuscript of the Liturgy of Egypt before the Council of Nicaea (325). The oldest document of this Alexandrine tradition is the Euchologion of Serapion of Thmuis (in the north). He became bishop before 339, and died between 353 and 360 AD. The text of this Euchologion has been preserved for us in a manuscript scribed in the eleventh century.[213]

Strong internal evidence indicates that the *Liturgy of Serapion* is copied from an Egyptian Eucharistic prayer, older than the time of Serapion. We can see the outline of this ancient Egyptian prayer by comparing it with other liturgical excerpts found in Egyptian books since the third century.[214]

We can see from the pro-anaphoral portions of *Liturgy of Serapion* (which he included in five parts) that the first part "directly repudiates the teaching of Arius that the Son does not know the essence of the Father." This draws us to the assumption that this first part was added to the pro-anaphoral portions of the Eucharist in

---

[212] Ignatius Aphrem II, *op. cit.*, 248.
[213] Dix, *op. cit.*, 162.
[214] Dix, *op. cit.*, 162.

Liturgy of Serapion during the first quarter of the fourth century, when the heresy of Arius was strongest.[215]

This pro-anaphora is:

> It is meet and right to praise, to hymn, to glorify thee the uncreated Father of the only-begotten Jesus Christ. We praise thee, uncreated God, who art unsearchable, ineffable, incomprehensible by any created substance. We praise thee who art known of thy Son, the only-begotten, who through him art spoken of and interpreted and made known to created nature. We praise thee who knowest the Son and revealest to the Saints the glories that are about him: who art known of thy begotten Word, and art brought to the sight and interpreted to the understanding of the Saints.[216]
>
> We praise thee, unseen Father, provider of immortality. Thou art the fount of life, the fount of light, the fount of all grace and all truth, lover of men, lover of the poor, who reconcilest thyself to all, and drawest all to thyself through the advent of thy beloved Son.[217]
>
> We beseech thee make us living men. Give us a spirit of light, that we may know thee the true [God] and him whom thou didst send, (even) Jesus Christ. Give us holy Spirit, that we may be able to tell forth and to enunciate thy unspeakable mysteries. May the Lord Jesus speak in us and holy Spirit, and hymn thee through us.[218]

---

[215] Dix, *op. cit.*, 165.
[216] Wordsworth, *Bishop Sarapion's Prayer Book*. (London: Society for Promoting Christian Knowledge, 1899), 60.
[217] Wordsworth, *op. cit.*, 60-61.
[218] Wordsworth, *op. cit.*, 61.

> For thou art far above all rule and authority and power and dominion, and every name that is named, not only in this world but also in that which is to come.[219]
>
> Beside thee stand thousand thousands and myriad myriads of angels, archangels, thrones, dominions, principalities, powers: by thee stand the two most honourable six-winged seraphim, with two wings covering the face, and with two the feet, and with two flying and crying holy, with whom receive also our cry of " holy " as we say...[220]

Development of the Liturgical Text of the Pro-Anaphora

The traditional preface to the Eucharistic prayer, as we have seen in the liturgy before Nicaea (mentioned above), is giving thanks to the Father through His Son Jesus Christ: "We offer You thanks O Lord, through Your beloved Son Jesus Christ..." This is the whole content of the Eucharist.

The preface to the *Liturgy of Serapion* deviates from this main principle, since it does not contain the word *thanks*, that is, *Eucharist*.[221]

A development occurred in the pro-anaphora, which diminished from the main purpose of this prayer, and that is offering thanks to God. The verbs of praise were prolonged and expanded such that the primary aim of thanksgiving was bypassed by verbs of singing, worshiping, and others. This same effect affected the congregation's response: "meet and right" (as we shall

---

[219] *Ibid.*
[220] *Ibid.*
[221] Dix, *op. cit.*, 165.

see shortly). Many additional attributes were added to the pro-anaphoral portion, attributes specific to the Person of the Father and the Person of the incarnate Son, attributes that show the unity of His Person and the qualities of His divine and human nature, which indicates confronting some heresies that appeared in the church, concerning the Trinity and the Incarnation.

Additionally, the Cherubic praise: "Holy, Holy, Holy…" was appended with, "Blessed is He who comes in the name of the Lord," in addition to the great litanies which we find in the *Liturgy of Mark*. These are the most important additions that overtook the pro-anaphoral portion.

What follows is an explanation of this development in the pro-anaphoral portion.

After the liturgical texts were established in the church, the abbreviated words exchanged between the priest and the congregation in the pro-anaphoral portion affected the liturgical script that follows immediately, giving it a stereotyped form, in which the priest or the congregation pick up the final words of the liturgical dialogue to begin with them a prayer or response. Thus, the prayer takes the form of a give and take between the celebrant priest and congregation. This is very clear in most holy prayers of the various anaphoras.

For example, the deacon's says, "You who are seated, **stand**," which the priest responds to with, "Before whom **stand** the angels, the archangels..."[222]

At the end of this prayer, the priest says, "praising continuously, without ceasing, saying – " and the people respond by saying, "Holy, holy, holy, Lord of hosts, heaven and earth are full of Your holy glory." The priest, in turn, responds saying, "Holy, holy, holy, indeed. O Lord our God..."[223]

The Eucharistic prayer begins in the *Didache*, and the *Apostolic Tradition* of Hippolytus, with a simple thanksgiving prayer: "We thank you" (Εὐχαριστοῦμεν).

In the popular form of the Anaphora, there were attempts to link between the verb "*thank*" and "*worthy and just*" (Ἄξιον καὶ δίκαιον), which is the last response in the pre-anaphoral dialogue.

In the *Liturgy of John Chrysostom* (347-407), the pro-anaphoral portion is,

> It is meet and right that we praise You (σὲ ὑμεῖν), bless You (σὲ εὐλογεῖν), extol You (σὲ αἰνεῖν), thank You (σοὶ εὐχαριστειν), worship You (σὲ προσκυνεῖν) in all places Your sovereignty... (ἐν παντὶ τόπῳ τῆς δεσποτείας σου).

This pro-anaphoral portion remains richer than the *Greek Liturgy of Basil*:

---

[222] H G Bishop Serapion, and H G Bishop Youssef., *op. cit.*, 184.
[223] The definition of *Anaphora* is the deliberate repetition of a word or phrase at the beginning of several successive verses, clauses, or paragraphs.

> You are the Master, Lord, God the Father, Pantocrator. It is meet and right and befitting Your holiness to **praise You, extol You, bless You, worship You, and thank You**. You Who the true God alone…

Here, the verbs of thanksgiving and praise are also five.

There are other Eastern examples that are longer and more abundant than the above Greek samples.[224]

The *Liturgy of Mark the Apostle* (Cyril) in the Coptic Church offers many more verbs of thanksgiving and praise than in any other liturgy, East and West:

> For truly it is fitting and right, and holy and becoming, and profitable to our souls, bodies, and spirits— O You, THE BEING, Master, Lord, God, the Father, the Pantocrator—at all times and in all places of Your dominion, to **praise** You, **hymn** You, **bless** You, **serve** You, **worship** You, **thank** You, and **glorify** You. And **confess** to You night and day, with incessant lips, with a heart that keeps not silent, and with unceasing doxologies…[225]

Here, the verbs of thanksgiving and praise are eight. We only find five in the *Liturgy of James the Apostle* in the Antiochian-Syriac rite:

> It is very meet right fitting and our bounden duty to praise thee, to bless thee, to celebrate thee, to worship thee, to give thanks to thee the creator of every creature visible and invisible whom the heavens and the heavens of heavens praise and all the hosts of them, the sun and the moon and all the choir of the stars, the earth and the sea and all that

---

[224] Baumstark, *op. cit.*, 88-89.
[225] H G Bishop Serapion, and H G Bishop Youssef, *op. cit.*, 335-336.

in them is, the heavenly Jerusalem, the church of the firstborn that are written in heaven, angels archangels princedoms powers thrones dominations virtues above the world, heavenly armies. The cherubin with many eyes, and the seraphin with six wings and with two of their wings they veil their face and with twain their feet and with twain they do fly one to another, with unceasing voices and unhushed theologies, a hymn of victory majesty and excellent glory with clear voice hymning, and crying and shouting and saying...[226]

Cyril of Jerusalem (315-386) comments of this preface in his Catechumen sermons:

After this, we make mention of heaven. and earth, and sea; of sun and moon; of stars and all the creation, rational and irrational, visible and invisible; of Angels, Archangels, Virtues, Dominions, Principalities, Powers, Thrones; of the Cherubim with many faces: in effect repeating that call of David's *Magnify the Lord with me*. We make mention also of the Seraphim, whom Esaias in the Holy Spirit saw standing around the throne of God, and with two of their wings veiling their face, and with twain their feet, while with twain they did fly, crying *Holy, Holy, Holy, is the Lord of Sabaoth*. For the reason of our reciting this confession of God, delivered down to us from the Seraphim, is this, that so we may be partakers with the hosts of the world above in their Hymn of praise.[227]

Although the *Coptic Liturgy of Basil* is void of verbs of praise, we find them five times in the *Coptic Liturgy of Gregory*:

We praise You, bless You, serve You, worship You, and glorify You.

---

[226] Brightman, *op. cit.*, 85-86.
[227] Cyril of Jerusalem, *Catechetical Lecture*, 23.

As for the *Liturgy of Serapion* (from the fourth century) the verbs of praise are only three:

It is meet and right to **praise**, to **hymn**, to **glorify**.

Thus, the *Coptic Liturgy of Mark* is distinct with the following verbs of praise:

Hymn You, serve You, and confess to You.

Two deacon responses are recited in this prayer. First, "You who are seated, stand," and second, "Look towards the East." There is also another response that immediately precedes the Cherubic praise: "Let us attend."

You who are seated, stand

The Church of Alexandria is distinct in that it has the deacon's response, "You who are seated, stand." In other liturgies, however, the call comes in as, "stand," or, "Let us stand."[228]

Naturally, this response does not mean that the people are seated, because the response before it is, "Stand in fear and look towards the East." The deacon's call, while we are standing on our feet, is to keep us attentive to receive the joy of spiritual alertness and not physical erectness.[229]

Look towards the East

---

[228] Ignatius Aphrem II, *op. cit.*, 192.
[229] Presbyter Samʿān Ibn Kalīl, *op. cit.*, 81.

This response came according to the *Greek Liturgy of Basil* as "Look towards the East always," (Εἰς ἀνατολὰς βλέπετε), using βλέπετε instead of βλέψατε. The East is the direction of the altar which should not part from our minds and hearts, whether we are in church or at work. Look towards the East always where there is the altar and the body and blood of Emmanuel our God placed on it, and the angels and archangels standing.

The church arranged for us to look toward the East before the Cherubic praise, because, after we have regained our honor through holy baptism, we approach praise with the esteem of children and gratitude of the redeemed.[230]

Let us attend

At the end of the preface to the offertory, and immediately before the Cherubic praise, the deacon says, "Let us attend," (Προσχῶμεν).

Some Coptic Euchologion manuscripts mentioned while others omitted this response. Although it is not mentioned in many of them,[231] it was

---

[230] Presbyter Samʿān Ibn Kalīl, *op. cit.*, 81.
[231] This response was not found in the Oxford Manuscript No. 17 (Coptic), which is the oldest complete Coptic-Arabic Euchologion manuscript scribed on 1288. It is also not found in the Library of the Monastery of Macarius Manuscripts No. 133, 136, 147 (Rites), nor in the Coptic Euchologion published by al-Tukhi in Rome in the seventeenth century, nor was it mentioned in the *Greek Liturgy of Mark* in the F. Kacmarcik Codex.

mentioned in some.[232] Its popularity in all liturgies came after the publication of the Euchologion (1902), where its practice predominated, and the other disappeared.

As for the deacon's response, "Let us attend," it is for each person to cease from all their preoccupations, to lift up the eyes of their mind to the Cherubim who are full of eyes, and for all to cry out once they hear this heavenly call, as Isaiah informed that, "*And one cried to another.*" At that point, the church must become silent briefly, to hear, intellectually, the praise of the Cherubim, joining with them with unceasing praise, "*Holy, holy, holy…*"[233]

In a Euchologion from the fourteenth century, this response was the following:

> Let us attend in silence and understanding. The heavenly hosts praise, and we likewise praise with them.[234]

Pro-anaphoral portion in the Liturgy of Mark (Cyril)

This prayer, which begins with the liturgical dialogue, "The Lord be with you all," and ends immediately before the Cherubic praise is short in the *Liturgy of Basil*, somewhat longer in the *Liturgy of Gregory*, and is very long in the *Liturgy of Mark*. A large number of litanies were added which split this prayer

---

[232] This response was found in the *Greek Liturgy of Basil* published by E. Renaudot, and in the Library of the Monastery of Macarius Manuscript No. 134 (Rites). It is known in the Greek Church Liturgies.
[233] Isaiah 6.3
[234] Presbyter Samʿān Ibn Kalīl, *op. cit.*, 81-82.

into two parts separated from each other in the *Liturgy of Mark*.

The pro-anaphoral portion in the *Liturgy of Mark* (in its first half) is interspersed with the three deacon's responses:

> You who are seated, stand,
>
> Look towards the East always,
>
> Let us attend.

The priest says,

> You are He who has created man according to Your own image and after Your likeness. And You have created everything through Your Wisdom — Your true Light, Your only-begotten Son, our Lord, God, Savior, and King of us all, Jesus Christ; through whom we give thanks and offer unto You, with Him and the Holy Spirit — the holy, co-essential, and indivisible Trinity — this rational sacrifice and this bloodless service.[235]

The priest signs the incense box, puts a spoonful of incense into the censer, takes it in his hands, and says:

> This [this rational sacrifice and this bloodless service], which all nations offer unto You.[236]

The priest signs the gifts on the altar with the censer, from East to West and from north to south, saying:

---

[235] H G Bishop Serapion, and H G Bishop Youssef, *op. cit.*, 336-337.
[236] *Ibid.*, 337.

.. from the East to the West and from the north to the south.[237]

Here, he offers incense over the gifts, saying,

> For great is Your name, O Lord, among all the nations; and in every place incense is offered unto Your holy name, and a pure sacrifice. And upon this sacrifice and this offering.[238]

Here, immediately comes the deacon's response,

> You who are seated, stand, and look towards the East.

However, the congregation's response, "Lord have mercy," is followed with fifteen litanies before continuing the pro-anaphoral portion that ends with the Cherubic praise:

> For You are God, who is above every principality and authority, every power and dominion, and every name that is named, not only in this age, but also in that which is to come.[239]

The following is a clear order that the *Liturgy of Mark* follows:

> **Litany:** (1) Peace, (2) Sick, (3) Travelers, (4) Waters of the River, or plants, or airs of heaven, and (5) King, (6) Commemoration and Diptych (equivalent to Litany of the departed)
>
> (7) Oblations, (8) Patriarch, (9) Bishops, (10) All Christians, (11) Place, (12) Those standing in this place, and (13) Those who asked us to pray for them

---

[237] *Ibid.*
[238] *Ibid.*
[239] H G Bishop Serapion, and H G Bishop Youssef., *op. cit.*, 373.

Deacon: "Worship God in fear and trembling."

(14) Celebrant priest (inaudible, beginning with, "Remember, O Lord, my weak and wretched soul").

(15) Priesthood

(15) Assemblies

Deacon: "You who are seated, stand,"

The litany which begins with, "Loose the bound," to which the people answer, "Lord have mercy," after each stanza.

Deacon: "And Look towards the East."

Priest: For You are God, who is above every principality and authority, every power and dominion, and every name that is named, not only in this age, but also in that which is to come… But with all that hallow You, receive from us—we too—our hallowing, O Lord, as we praise You with them, saying—

Deacon: Let us attend.

People: Holy, holy, holy, Lord of hosts…

The massive amount of litanies, which was appended to the *Liturgy of Mark*, split the pro-anaphoral portion into two: 1) this preface, which offers thanksgiving, offered to God through His Son Jesus Christ; and 2) these fifteen litanies (if we consider the commemoration and diptych equivalent to a litany for the departed), which are among the most important additions to the pro-anaphoral portion of the *Liturgy of Mark*, by Cyril of Alexandria (412-444).

In the *Liturgies of Basil and Cyril*, they each maintained a coherent pro-anaphoral portion, where the litanies appear in them towards the end, after the descent of the Holy Spirit on us and on the oblations. This development overtook the position of the litanies in the liturgies, in general, during the fourth century.

The litany in the *Liturgy of Serapion* specific to the living and the departed, and those offering the oblations, were appended to the original text of the Eucharistic prayer after the preparation prayer; this was "before the end of the fourth century."[240]

The churches sought to insert the litanies into the Eucharistic prayer after the oblations become the body and precious blood of Christ so that our supplications may receive their strength and effectiveness from the sacrifice placed on the altar.[241]

This endeavour first appeared in the Church of Jerusalem during the third century, where this actually took place. We find a spiritual liturgical exposition on this, thereafter, in the sermons of Cyril of Jerusalem (315-386), more precisely in 348.[242]

Until that time, this liturgical development had not reached the *Egyptian Liturgy of Serapion*. The church of Alexandria adopted a different mindset,[243] having received it from the text of her liturgical prayers, which

---

[240] Dix, *op. cit.*, 170.
[241] *Ibid.*, 171.
[242] *Ibid.*
[243] *Ibid.*

says that the bread and wine placed on the altar are holies previously placed before the Lord on the altar.[244] In the pro-anaphoral portion of the *Liturgy of Mark* (in its first half to be precise) the liturgical text says,

> For great is Your name, O Lord, among all the nations… And upon this **sacrifice** and this offering.

After the priest says, "Holy," he continues,

> Fill this, Your **sacrifice**, O Lord, with the blessing, which is from You, by the coming down upon it of Your Holy Spirit.[245]

He adds, in the past tense,

> Your precious gifts which **are already set forth before You**, this bread and this cup…[246]

And also,

> You are He before whose holy glory we have put Your own gifts, from what is Your own, O our holy Father.[247]

These are all signs that refer to the offertory rite, which was preserved by the Egyptian church, a mysterious rite lost in other churches. Therefore, the litanies were attached in the *Liturgy of Mark* to the pro-anaphoral portion, prior to the Cherubic praise. We also find that the litanies in the *Liturgy of Serapion of Thmuis* in the fourth century come at the beginning, before the pro-anaphoral portion begins.

---

[244] *Ibid.*
[245] H G Bishop Serapion, and H G Bishop Youssef., *op. cit.*, 376.
[246] *Ibid.*, 377.
[247] *Ibid.*, 382.

There are evident differences in these litanies between the churches. The Church of Rome appended these litanies onto the Eucharistic prayer preface, but following the Cherubic praise (except for the litany for the departed, which was attached to the end of the liturgy). In the Church in Odessa, these litanies are prior to the sanctification.

In general, what distinguishes the Alexandrine rite from the Antiochian rite is that the litanies in the Alexandrine tradition come at the beginning, such as in the *Liturgy of Mark and Serapion*, but in the Antiochian tradition liturgies it comes at the end, as in the *Coptic Liturgies of Basil and Gregory*.

CHERUBIC PRAISE

Introduction

The words of the Cherubic praise are:

Holy, Holy, Holy, Lord of hosts, heaven and earth are full of Your holy glory.[248]

The Latin liturgical term for this Cherubic praise, known in all churches, is *Sanctus*, which means in Latin, "Holy."

The first part of this praise, "Holy, Holy, Holy, Lord of hosts," is derived verbatim from Isaiah the Prophet: *"Holy, holy, holy is the Lord of hosts; the whole earth is full of His glory!"*[249] There is a slight alteration with the phrase, "*the whole earth is* full *of His* glory." The liturgical text is "*heaven and earth are* full *of Your holy* glory," as Jeremiah the Prophet says, *"'Do I not fill heaven and earth?' says the Lord."*[250] Thus, the praise becomes in the second person, "Your glory," and not the third person, "His glory."

The Church of Alexandria is the Origin of the Cherubic Praise

---

[248] H G Bishop Serapion, and H G Bishop Youssef., *op. cit.*, 185.
[249] Isaiah 6.3
[250] Jeremiah 23.24

This praise first originated in the Egyptian Church and from there it spread to the whole Christian world.[251]

The pro-anaphora text of Serapion, which precedes the Cherubic praise, is comparable to that found in the anaphora of Mark the Apostle. Hence, the *Liturgy of Serapion* originates from an ancient Egyptian liturgical prayer, greatly resembling that from which was derived the *Liturgy of Mark the Apostle*.[252]

Below is a comparison between the two liturgical texts (which precede the Cherubic praise) in the *Liturgies of Mark and Serapion*:

Liturgy of Serapion	Liturgy of Mark
For thou art far above all rule and authority and power and dominion, and every name that is named, not only in this world but also in that which is to come.	For You are God, who is above every principality and authority, every power and dominion, and every name that is named, not only in this age, but also in that which is to come.
Beside thee stand thousand thousands and myriad myriads of angels, archangels, thrones, dominions, principalities, powers:	You are He before whom stand thousands of thousands and ten thousand times ten thousand of holy angels and archangels, serving You.
By thee stand the two most honourable six-winged seraphim,	You are He before whom stand Your two most honored living creatures, with their six wings

---

[251] Dix, *op. cit.*, 165.
[252] Dix, *op. cit.*, 165.

With two wings covering the face, and with two the feet, and with two flying	and many eyes, the seraphim and the cherubim.
And crying holy,	With two wings they cover their faces on account of Your divinity that cannot be beheld or comprehended, and with two they cover their feet, and with the other two they fly.
With whom receive also our cry of "holy" as we say:[253]	
	For at all times, every thing hallows You.
	But with all that hallow You, receive from us—we too—our hallowing, O Lord, as we praise You with them, saying—[254]
"Holy, holy, holy, Lord of hosts, heaven and earth are full of Your holy glory."[255]	

Gregory Dix affirms:

> We note only that the use of the sanctus at the Alexandrian eucharist, preceded by a preface closely resembling that of Serapion, can be traced in the writings of Origen at Alexandria A.D. 230. This is the earliest evidence of the use of this hymn in the liturgy.[256]

The inclusion of this praise in the writing of Clement of Rome and Tertullian (160-225) does not necessitate that this Cherubic praise is an ecclesiastic chant sung within the Eucharist.[257]

---

[253] Wordsworth, *op. cit.*, 61.
[254] H G Bishop Serapion, and H G Bishop Youssef., *op. cit.*, 373-374.
[255] *Ibid.*, 375.
[256] Dix, *op. cit.*, 165.
[257] *Ibid.*

Clement of Rome says in his Letter to the Corinthians:[258]

> Let our boasting and our confidence be in Him. Let us submit ourselves to His will. Let us consider the whole multitude of His angels, how they stand ever ready to minister to His will. For the Scripture saith, "Ten thousand times ten thousand stood around Him, and thousands of thousands ministered unto Him, and cried, Holy, holy, holy, [is] the Lord of Sabaoth; the whole creation is full of His glory."[259] And let us therefore, conscientiously gathering together in harmony, cry to Him earnestly, as with one mouth, that we may be made partakers of His great and glorious promises.[260]

Clement of Rome's words do not indicate that this praise is said within the Eucharistic prayer, because, until that time, it was not a liturgical response.[261]

Likewise, Tertullian (160-225) in his *On Prayer* comments on this Biblical praise with touching words:

> He to whom that surrounding circle of angels cease not to say, "Holy, Holy, Holy?" In likewise, therefore, we too, candidates for angelhood, if we succeed in deserving it, begin even here on earth to learn by heart that strain hereafter to be raised unto God.[262]

---

[258] Writing towards the end of the first century.
[259] Daniel 7.10; Isaiah 6.3
[260] *ANF01*, 24 (Chapter 24).
[261] Dix, *op. cit.*, 165.
[262] *ANF03*, 995 (On Prayer, 3).

These words by Tertullian, even until that time, do not point to a liturgical response said inside the liturgy.[263]

The Cherubic praise is missing in the *Liturgy of Hippolytus*, it was a praise unknown to the Roman Church even until that point in time. It is also missing in the oldest liturgical documents.[264]

Here it becomes clear to us that the use of the pro-anaphora, which is immediately followed by the Cherubic praise, first appeared in the Church of Alexandria before 230, and from there spread to all Egyptian churches, and thenceforth to all the corners of the world.[265]

The Cherubic praise is an authentic Egyptian element derived from the Church of Jerusalem,[266] as Cyril of Jerusalem (315-386) refers to it in his twenty-third sermon.[267]

John Chrysostom (347-407) mentioned it more than once in his writings as an established rite in the Church of Antioch. Among the early Syrian documents from which we are acquainted with the presence of this praise in the Church of Antioch is the *Works by John Chrysostom*. This is a Christian fiction ethical book from the fourth century in which we encounter the words of

---

[263] Dix, *op. cit.*, 165.
[264] *Ibid.*
[265] Dix, *op. cit.*, 165.
[266] *Ibid.*, 196-197.
[267] *NPNF2-07*, 293 (Lecture 23.6).

this praise, which was used in the consecration prayers of water and oil before baptism. It says,

> O Almighty Lord, allow for your Holy Spirit to come on this oil, and on this water... Yes Lord, bless this water with Your voice echoed over the Jordan." It continues saying, "And in that hour, fire hovered over the oil and flapped its wings of the angels over the oil. And all those present cried out, men women and children: Holy, Holy, Holy Lord Almighty, heaven and earth are full of Your praise.

Athanasius of Alexandria (328-373) witnesses that the use of the Cherubic praise has spread throughout all the churches. In *On the Trinity*, he mentions that the churches of Christ from East to West confess in the Eucharist that the Cherubim rightly honor the Father.

Gregory Dix (1901-1952) also sees that the preface to the Eucharist which precedes the Cherubic praise is of Alexandrine origin and was derived from the Church of Jerusalem,[268] or to be specific, the *Liturgy of James the Brother of the Lord* retrieved it from the *Liturgy of Mark*.

> The third century Alexandrian writer Origen in treating of the two seraphim in Isaiah vi., in close connection with the eucharistic preface and sanctus, makes it clear that he interprets Isaiah vi. 2 as meaning that the two seraphim 'had each six wings; with twain he covered the Face *of God* and with twain he covered the Feet *of God* and with twain the seraph (itself) did fly.'[269]

This is exactly what we find in the preface to the *Liturgy of Serapion*:

---

[268] Dix, *op. cit.*, 196-197.
[269] *Ibid.*, 197.

> By thee stand the two most honourable six-winged seraphim, with two wings covering the face (Τὸ πρόσωπον – To Prosopon), and with two the feet, and with two flying.[270]

During the time of Athanasius of Alexandria (328-373), the Church of Alexandria had modified "Τὸ πρόσωπον" (the face) into "Τὰ πρόσωπα" (their faces). This is what we find in the *Liturgy of James the Brother of the Lord* and also what John Chrysostom (347-407) emphasized in Antioch at the end of the fourth century.[271]

Cyril of Jerusalem, like Serapion, continued to keep the ancient interpretation of the Church of Alexandria, which appeared in the third century. From this, we learned that the Church of Jerusalem retrieved the preface and the sanctus from the Church of Alexandria.[272]

Development of the Sanctus in the Various Churches

In the Greek text of the *Coptic Liturgy of Basil*, published by E. Renaudot, the response is "Holy, Holy, Holy Lord of Hosts,"[273] without any additions. This is the response in its extremely ancient form.

In the *Liturgy of Serapion*, the response is: "Holy, Holy, Holy, Lord of Sabaoth, full is the heaven and the

---

[270] Wordsworth, *op. cit.*, 61.
[271] Dix, *op. cit.*, 197.
[272] *Ibid.*, 197.
[273] *PG.*, 31, 1636C.

earth of thy glory," without describing this *glory*. The priest recollects his words from the congregation's words to add, "Full is the heaven, full also is the earth of thy excellent glory."[274]

This is exactly what we find in the Balayza Monastery manuscript, which renders a portion of the Greek text of the *Liturgy of Mark*. It mentions the response without describing the glory of the Lord, which fills heaven and earth:

> Holy, Holy, Holy, Lord of Sabaoth; heaven and earth are full of Thy holy glory.

It is worth noting that *All-Holy* describes this glory, but is not found in the Byzantine rite, as in the *Liturgy of John Chrysostom*.

The rites of Jerusalem, Antioch, Byzantium, and Rome add, after the Sanctus,

> Hosanna in the highest. Blessed is He that cometh in the name of the Lord.[275]

In the *Syrian Liturgy of James the Brother of the Lord*, this praise is:

> Holy, Holy, Holy, mighty Lord God of Sabaoth, of the glory and honour of whose majesty heaven and earth are full. Hosanna in the highest, blessed is He that came and cometh in the name of the Lord, Hosanna in the highest.[276]

---

[274] Wordsworth, *op. cit.*, 61-62.
[275] Dix, *op. cit.*, 188,514.
[276] Brightman, *op. cit.*, 86.

This exact rendering is found in the *Coptic Liturgy of Gregory* in Greek,[277] and is also mentioned in the Euchologion Manuscript No. 155 (Rite) in the Library of the Monastery of Macarius, which contains the Greek text of the *Liturgy of Gregory*. This rendering is also found in the Apostles' Liturgy, known as the Liturgy of the two apostles Addai and Mari.[278] These churches explain blending these two chants, heaven and earth, angels and humans, as a sign that heaven and earth are united by Christ's incarnation and redemption: the angels and humans make up one church whose Head is Christ the God-Man, and so,

> At the name of Jesus every knee should bow, of those in heaven, and of those on earth, and of those under the earth.[279]

The origin of adding the blessing, "Blessed…," to the Sanctus is found in the *Apostolic Constitutions of Syrian Rites* where the Sanctus is,

> Holy, holy, holy Lord of Host, heaven and earth are full of Your glory. Blessed are You forever. Amen.

Book VII of the *Apostolic Constitutions* mentions a blessing prayer derived from the Jewish prayers:

> The holy Seraphim, together with the six-winged cherubin, sing to Thee the triumphal hymn, and cry with voice unceasing, 'Holy, holy, holy is the Lord of Hosts; heaven and earth are full of Thy glory.' And the other multitudes of the orders, angels, archangels, thrones, dominions,

---

[277] Burmester, O.H.E. *The Greek Kirugmatat, op. cit.,* 376.
[278] Brightman, *op. cit.,* 284; Dix, *op. cit.,* 179.
[279] Philippians 2.10

principalities, authorities, powers, cry aloud and say, 'Blessed be the glory of the Lord from His place.'[280]

The words of this praise concur with the morning prayers of the Jewish Synagogue, which relates to the verses in Ezekiel,

Blessed by the glory of the Lord from his place.[281]

Thus, this Jewish text is the first to combine the Cherubic Praise, "*Holy*," with the appended part, "*Blessed*," which is familiar to some rites until this day. Liturgists see that this connection has origins also in the *Book of Enoch* (39:9-14), written in the second century BC. It was popular in Christian circles in the first three centuries:

> In those days I praised and extolled the name of the Lord of Spirits with blessings and praises... saying: 'Blessed is He, and may He be blessed from the beginning and for evermore... Those who sleep not bless Thee: they stand before Thy glory and bless, praise, and extol, saying: "Holy, holy, holy, is the Lord of Spirits: He filleth the earth with spirits."' And here my eyes saw all those who sleep not: they stand before Him and bless and say: 'Blessed be Thou, and blessed be the name of the Lord for ever and ever.'

From this it becomes clear to us that the Sanctus was popular and known in the early Christian literature. Its first use in the liturgy was in the Church of Alexandria, and more specifically in the *Liturgy of Mark and Serapion*.[282]

---

[280] Warren, *op. cit.*, 266-267.
[281] Merzbacher, L, ed. *The Order of Prayer for Divine Service*. (New York: Thalmessinger & Cahn, 1863), 67; Ezekiel 3.12.
[282] Dix, *op. cit.*, 165.

The Euchologion (1902) contains six *Aspasmos Watos*:

1) "Come to the table, to bless God, with the angels and archangels, crying out and saying..." (Ⲇⲉⲩⲧⲉ ⲓⲥ ⲑⲏⲛ ⲧ⎕ⲣⲁⲡⲉⲍⲁⲛ ...).[288]

2) "Glory be to You O Father, glory to You who are one with the Holy Spirit, one God, one Lord..." (Ⲇⲟⲝⲁ ⲥⲓ ⲱ⎕ Ⲡⲁⲧⲉⲣ . Ⲇⲟⲝⲁ ⲥⲓ ⲱ ⲙⲟⲛⲟⲅⲉⲛⲏⲥ ...).

3) "The Cherubim worship Him, the Seraphim glorify Him, crying out and saying, the Holy, holy, holy..." (Ⲧⲁ ⲭⲉⲣⲟⲩⲃⲓⲙ ⲡ⎕ⲣⲟⲥⲕⲩⲛⲟⲛ ⲁⲩⲧⲟⲛ ...).

4) "Let us praise with the angels, and the heavenly hosts, which is the Father, Son, and Holy Spirit..." (Ⲙⲁⲣⲉⲛϩⲱⲥ ⲛⲉⲙ ⲛⲓⲁⲅⲅⲉⲗⲟⲥ ...).

5) "The Cherubim worship You, the Seraphim glorify You, crying out and saying" (Ⲛⲓⲭⲉⲣⲟⲩⲃⲓⲙ ⲥⲉⲟⲩⲱϣⲧ ⲙ⎕ⲙⲟⲕ ...).[289]

---

[288] This *Aspasmos* was mentioned by Ibn Kabar (d. 1324) as one that is chanted during the Great Fast, Kioak, and the Apostles Fast; therefore, it was labeled, *First Aspasmos Watos,* and not, *Annual Aspasmos Watos,* as Euchologion (1902) mentions. This shows clearly that many *Aspasmos Watos*, which were added for the various church occasions are more recent while this ancient *Aspasmos* fell back and is no longer recited.

[289] This is the *Aspasmos* which was appended to the introduction of the Sanctus. It is perhaps the shortest abbreviated *Aspasmos Watos*; however, there is a greater possibility that it is the only annual *Aspasmos* mentioned by Ibn Kabar (d. 1324). As such, it is among the oldest *Aspasmos Watos*.

6) "The Cherubim, Seraphim, angels, archangels, thrones, dominions, principalities, authorities, powers, cry aloud and say"[290] (Ⲛⲓⲭⲉⲣⲟⲩⲃⲓⲙ ⲛⲉⲙ ⲛⲓⲥⲉⲣⲁⲫⲓⲙ ...).

Finally, it is beneficial for you to know that Anba Severus Ibn al-Muqaffaʿ Bishop of al-Ashmūnīn (~915-1000) mentions the text of this Cherubic praise, then comments on it:

> ... and after the Gospel, [the priest] hallows God with the angels, as the priest says: "You are He before whom stand the angels, the many-eyes cherubim and the six-winged seraphim, praising You continuously without ceasing saying." All those in the church answer him with one voice saying, "Holy, holy, holy, Lord of Host, heaven and earth are full of Your holy glory." This sanctification is said by all those present in the church, sanctifying God the Trinity with this Sanctus. He likewise sanctifies them of their sins, as He said on the tongue of Isaiah the Prophet: "I will glorify those who glorify me, and I will hallow those who hallow me." By this hallow, the believer is sanctified of his sins. By saying is sanctified means being purified of sins. *Taqdees* (sanctification) is a Syrian and Hebrew term meaning purification. Sanctification is purification. The Holy is pure. Understand this terminology also, to comprehend that sanctification purifies the believer of his sins.[291]

---

[290] Warren, *op. cit.*, 276.
[291] Ibn al-Muqaffaʿ, Sāwīris. *The Precious Jewel in Clarifying Religion* (Al-Dur al-Thamīn fī Iʿīdāh al-Dīn), 124.

HOLY, HOLY, HOLY

Elucidation

After the people end the Sanctus, "*Holy, holy, holy, Lord of Hosts...*" the priest immediately begins praying.

In the *Liturgy of Basil*, he says:

> Holy, holy, holy, indeed. O Lord our God, who formed us, created us, and placed us in the Paradise of joy...[292]

Here he recounts the narrative of the Creation and Fall, the Incarnation of the Son of God in the last days for our salvation, His death, descent into Hades, Resurrection from the dead, ascension to heaven, and His Second Coming to living and the dead.

The congregation responds:

> According to Your mercy, O Lord, and not according to our sins.[293]

In the *Liturgy of Gregory* he says:

> Holy, holy, O Lord, and holy are You in everything, and most excellent is the light of Your essence....[294]

Here he digresses in describing the Creation of man, heaven, earth, and everything in them, the Fall of

---

[292] H G Bishop Serapion, and H G Bishop Youssef., *op. cit.*, 187.
[293] *Ibid.*, 189.
[294] *Ibid.*, 269.

man by eating of the tree of knowledge of good and evil, the Coming of God the Son the Omnipresent to us on earth for our salvation, His enduring the Passion and being slain, and proclaiming His Second Coming to judge the living and the dead and give each one according to his deeds.

The congregation respond:

According to Your mercy, O Lord, and not according to our sins.[295]

There are shared characteristics between this part of the *Liturgy of Gregory the Theologian* and in the *Apostolic Constitutions*, which were written in the second half of the fourth century:

Apostolic Constitutions	Liturgy of Gregory the Theologian[296]
You made heaven like a dome, and spread it like a tent, and set the earth upon nothing.	You have raised heaven as a roof for me, and established the earth for me to walk upon.
You have encircled the great depth, and enclosed it with a great limit.	For my sake, You have bound the sea.
You filled your world, and adorned it with herbs that smell good and healing, and with many and varied animals.	For my sake, You have manifested the nature of animals.
I planted a paradise in Eden to the east. She adorned it with all	And opened for me Paradise to enjoy, and have given to me the learning of Your knowledge.

---

[295] H G Bishop Serapion, and H G Bishop Youssef., *op. cit.*, 274.
[296] *Ibid.*, 269-270.

edible plants, and brought it into it as well as into a very luxurious dwelling. And when I made him, I gave him a law planted in him, that he might have and in himself the seed of divine knowledge. And when you brought him to the paradise of bliss, you gave him authority over everything, forbidding him only to taste from one tree.	You have manifested to me the tree of life… Of one plant have You forbidden me to eat.

In the *Liturgy of Mark* he says:

> Holy, O Lord of hosts, heaven and earth are full of Your holy glory, O Lord our God. Truly, heaven and earth are full of Your holy glory through Your only-begotten Son, our Lord, God, Savior, and King of us all, Jesus Christ. Fill this, Your sacrifice, O Lord, with the blessing, which is from You, by the coming down upon it of Your Holy Spirit. And with blessing, bless. And with sanctification, sanctify — Your precious gifts which are already set forth before You, this bread and this cup.[297]

The congregation's response, "According to Your mercy, O Lord, and not according to our sins,"[298] does not come in this place in the *Liturgy of Mark*, but is recited later. It comes after the priest declares the Second Coming of the only-begotten Son at the end of this age to judge the world in justice and give each one according to his works, if good or if evil.

Explanation and Comment

---

[297] H G Bishop Serapion, and H G Bishop Youssef., *op. cit.*, 376-377.
[298] *Ibid.*, 189.

Now we need to search in the ancient Coptic manuscripts for these parts of the Divine Liturgy. By searching, we find that, whether in the Coptic text or the Greek text, the priest begins by saying, "Holy," whether once (as in the *Liturgy of Mark*), or three times (as in the *Coptic Liturgies of Basil and Gregory*), without the current introduction that the priest says, "Holy, Holy, Holy," accompanied by signings.

Here, two things become clear:

1) The ancient Euchologion manuscripts, and our ancient ritual books, mention that the priest prays, "Holy..." immediately after the Sanctus, without being preceded with "Holy," three times, as occurs in contemporary liturgies.

2) There is no mention of any signings in this part of the liturgy. This is also what I have previously mentioned regarding the liturgical dialogue that begins in the Anaphora. The Vatican Manuscript No. 17 (Coptic) and Oxford Manuscript No. 360 (Huntington) do not mention anything about these signings. Although not mentioned, these rites may have been transmitted to us through the oral tradition. Ibn Sebāʿ (thirteenth century) does not mention anything about them either, despite his attention to detail in describing the minutest ritualistic details in the liturgy.[299]

In fact, we are before an inconsistent ritual practice that has thrived in some churches while not in

---

[299] Yoḥanna Ibn A'bī Zakaria Ibn Sebāʿ, *op. cit.*, 248.

others. Over time, one of these practices prevailed and spread, while the others disappeared. We are also before a ritual change that does not come naturally from the content of the prayers and their liturgical words but are in some ritual practices accompanying this liturgical text.

The first mention of these signings is found in the writings of Pope Gabriāl V (1409-1427) in his *Ritual Order*. However, this rite is concurrent with the congregation chanting, "Holy, Holy, Holy," in the introduction to the Sanctus, and not while the priest says, "Holy." This is also what Euchologion (1902) mentions.

Concerning this part, we read in Euchologion (1902) what the priest says and does in the *Liturgy of Mark*:

> The priest takes the cloth which is on the chalice on his right hand, and when the people say *Holy*, he signs three times: firstly, on himself, secondly, on the servants, and thirdly, on the people, while the fellow priest circles the altar with the censer. Then the priest says: 'Holy, O Lord of hosts, heaven and earth are full of Your holy glory…'[300]

This is also what we find in the *Liturgy of Gregory*, mentioned also in Euchologion (1902):

> The congregation may chant the following *Aspasmos Watos* hymn 'Come to the table, to bless God (ⲇⲉⲩⲧⲉ ⲓⲥ ⲑⲏⲛ ⲧ⳿ⲡⲁⲛⲉⲍⲁ …), or another Aspasmos. Yet, this is before they say the previous 'ⲁ̀ⲅⲓⲟⲥ.'[301]

---

[300] Cf. H G Bishop Serapion, and H G Bishop Youssef., *op. cit.*, 376.
[301] This is the Sanctus.

He continues,

> Here the priest makes the sign of the cross on himself, the deacons, and the congregation, saying, "Holy, holy, O Lord, and holy are You in everything…"[302]

This is exactly what Pope Gabriāl V mentions stressing that the priest signs these three times while the people chant the Sanctus:

> When he reaches where they say, 'Holy, holy, holy,' he also signs three times, first on himself, second on the serving deacon, and third on the people.[303]

As for the *Liturgy of Basil* (most frequently used), Euchologion (1902) added instructions, not found in the writings of Pope Gabriāl V, by saying:

> The priest places the cloth in his right hand on the altar, transfers to his left hand the cloth which he is holding in his right hand. He takes in his right hand the cloth that is upon the chalice, and with it makes the sign of the cross three times; saying ⲁⲅⲓⲟⲥ each time: firstly, upon himself, his face being turned towards the East, then upon the deacons on his right hand, and lastly towards the West, upon the people. If there is a fellow priest, he circles the altar with the censer. Then the priest says: "Holy, holy, holy, indeed. O Lord our God…"[304]

Here it becomes clear that Euchologion (1902) adopted ritual practices that vary from those mentioned by Pope Gabriāl V (1409-1427) in his *Ritual Order*. The deviations in Euchologion (1902) are:

---

[302] H G Bishop Serapion, and H G Bishop Youssef., *op. cit.*, 267-269.
[303] Pope Gabriāl V, *op. cit.*, 77.
[304] Cf. H G Bishop Serapion, and H G Bishop Youssef., *op. cit.*, 187.

- The signings are to be made while the priest says Holy (agios) in Greek, not while the congregation say the Sanctus, as the priest says *Holy* trice in Greek and then repeats it in Coptic or Arabic.

- The signings are made with the chalice cloth (after moving the cloths around).

- The second signing is to the priest's right only, not on the deacons on the left and right of the altar.

- The accompanying priest circles the altar, as in the *Liturgy of Cyril*.

Perhaps this was a rite passed down to us through oral tradition, and was first documented in Euchologion (1902) by Hegumen ʿAbd al-Massīh Salīb al-Massʿūdī al-Baramūsī (1848-1935).

Meditation on the Signings with the Offertory Cloth, and then with the Chalice Cloth

The current ritual practiced is that at the beginning of the Anaphora, three signings are to be made with the offertory cloth, first on the congregation, second on the deacons, and third on the priest himself. As for the three signings that occur thereafter with the chalice cloth, they are first on the priest, second on the deacons, and third on the congregation.

The offertory signings begin with the congregation, for whom the Lamb came carrying the sins of the world to save us, to be our Emmanuel, God with us. Thus, this signing agrees with the priest's words to the congregation, "The Lord be with you."

The signings done with the chalice cloth begin with the priest because the High Priest was first stained with the blood on the cross, so His blood flowed as a purification and sanctification for a congregation the Lord willed to purchase for Himself.

During the previous signings, the Lamb was uncovered while the signings were with the Lamb cloth (while the chalice was covered) because after the reconciliation through the Lord's resurrection, He appeared to the church (in the person of Mary Magdalene) who was not able to recognize Him, at first. However, the chalice and Lamb have been unveiled, now, as the Lord revealed Himself to His glorious church.

The signings with the chalice cloth is symbolic of the sanctification that occurred by the blood of our Lord Jesus Christ, who offered for us a superior sacrifice. When the priest signs himself, he gains the inner strength of sanctification by the sign of the cross and the blood of Christ. When he signs the deacons, all gain the strength of an everlasting life and all those around the altar say, *Holy*. When he turns to the West, signing the people, each person signs himself also, because once *Holy* is said, even if in private prayer, each person signs

Mozarabic rite. Likewise, the Byzantine liturgy also begins with *Holy,* yet it is preceded by an expression that recounts the words of the angelic hosts:

> With these blessed hosts, O Master, the Philanthropist, we also chant saying, 'You are Holy and holy in everything...'

The prayer continues in narrating the story of salvation beginning with the creation, fall, incarnation, passion, resurrection from the death, ascension to heaven, and sitting at the right hand of the Father, ending with the second coming from heaven for judgment. Afterwards, the congregation respond:

> According to Your mercy, O Lord, and not according to our sins.

According to Paris Manuscript No. 235 (Greek), published by E. Renaudot, we find that in the Greek text the segment that begins with, "Holy, holy, holy, truly O Lord our God..." is joined to the segment immediately following it: "He incarnated and took flesh," without the response, "Amen," or, "Truly I believe," which divides this passage into three segments. Thus, the meaning is:

> ...Who of the Holy Spirit, and of the Virgin St. Mary incarnate and took flesh... and descended to Hades through the cross, and rose from the dead...

We can also find this order in Vatican Manuscript No. 17 (Coptic). The *Amen* response does not exist, but the priest continues his prayer:

> ...Who of the Holy Spirit, and of the Virgin St. Mary incarnate and took flesh and taught us the ways of salvation, and granted us birth...

The priest continues in prayer without any responses from the congregation until the response,

> According to Your mercy, O Lord, and not according to our sins.

The response, "Truly I believe" (ⲀⲘⲎⲚ ϯⲚⲀϨϯ), which separates between the priest's words, "He descended into Hades through the cross," and, "He arose from the dead...," is also not found either in Vatican Manuscript No. 17 (Coptic). Notice, that this response is said in the singular, while the other responses are all said in the plural since all responses are chanted by the congregation and not one person. This liturgical prayer order is also found in Oxford Manuscript No. 360 (Huntington).

The phrase, "He made us unto Himself an assembled people,"[309] means, "a special people." *Assembled* (περιούσιον) is a word with a long history in the Old Testament, as in, "*a people for Himself, a special treasure above all the peoples on the face of the earth.*"[310] This specialty is expressed by περιούσιον, which is often found in the Old Testament.

Afterwards, the liturgy progresses into the institution narrative, which begin in the *Coptic Liturgy of Basil* by the priest's words, "He instituted for us this great mystery of godliness..."[311], or, "I offer You, O my

---

[309] H G Bishop Serapion, and H G Bishop Youssef., *op. cit.*, 188.
[310] Deuteronomy 7.6.
[311] H G Bishop Serapion, and H G Bishop Youssef., *op. cit.*, 189.

Master, the symbols of my freedom..."[312] in the *Liturgy of Gregory*.

This **first feature**, narrating the history of salvation is found in the Byzantine rite, as in the *Liturgy of John Chrysostom*, but with greater brevity, as the priest says,

> ... Who (the only-begotten Son) when He had come and fulfilled all the economy for us, on the night that He gave up Himself ...

We find this feature also in the Liturgy of the Church of Antioch, primarily represented by the *Liturgy of James the Brother of the Lord*, where a more elaborate narrative of the history of salvation is found:

> Even as in truth thou art holy, King of the worlds and giver of all holiness, and holy also is thine only-begotten Son our Lord and God and Saviour Jesus Christ and holy also is thine Holy Spirit who searcheth all things, even the deep things of thee, God and Father. For holy art thou all-sovereign almighty terrible good, of fellow feeling and especially as touching thy creature: who madest man out of earth and gavest him delight in paradise: but when he transgressed thy commandment and fell thou didst not pass him by nor forsake him, O good, but didst chasten him as an exceeding merciful father: thou calledst him by the law, thou didst lead him by the prophets and last of all didst send thine only-begotten Son into the world that he might renew thine image: who, when he had come down and been incarnate of the Holy Ghost and of the holy mother of God and ever-virgin Mary and conversed with men and done all things for the redemption of our race...[313]

---

[312] *Ibid.*, 274.
[313] Brightman, *op. cit.*, 86.

The second feature is clearly visible in the original Coptic rite apart from all the rites, represented in the *Liturgy of Mark* (Cyril) and the *Liturgy of Serapion*: the Sanctus is immediately followed by the institution narrative without any narration of the history of salvation. However, the prelude into the words of the institution is preceded by a short expression that links the Sanctus and the institution.

In the *Liturgy of Mark*, this is expressed as:

> ...Truly, heaven and earth are **full** of Your holy glory through Your only-begotten Son, our Lord, God, Savior, and King of us all, Jesus Christ. **Fill** this, Your sacrifice, O Lord, with the blessing, which is from You, by the coming down upon it of Your Holy Spirit. And with blessing, bless. And with sanctification, sanctify— Your precious gifts which are already set forth before You, this bread and this cup.[314]

This transition appears clearest in the Balayza Monastery manuscript, where, after the priest says,

> Holy, holy, holy, Lord of Hosts, heaven and earth are full of Your glory,

He continues,

> **Fill** us also with Your glory and please send Your Holy Spirit...

This is also what we find in the *Liturgy of Serapion*. Immediately after the Sanctus, the priest says,

---

[314] H G Bishop Serapion, and H G Bishop Youssef., *op. cit.*, 376-377.

Heaven and earth are **full** of Your very fearful glory. O Lord of Host, **fill** also this sacrifice with Your might and fellowship, because we have offered this living sacrifice, a bloodless sacrifice.[315]

Here we find that the Alexandrine rite transitions from praising the Lord's glory which **fills** heaven and earth, to requesting **filling** the sacrifice with blessing, in preparation for the words of the institution, immediately, sanctifying the bread and wine.

In the *Liturgy of Mark*: "**Fill** (πλήρωσον) this, Your sacrifice, O Lord, with the blessing," or in the *Liturgy of Serapion*, "**Fill** (πλήρωσον) also this sacrifice with Your might and fellowship," is one of the distinct features of the Alexandrine liturgy.

Sanctifying the sacrifice, according to the *Liturgy of Mark*, is through the blessing of the Father through the descent of the Holy Spirit upon it. Therefore, the priest says, "**Fill** this, Your sacrifice, O Lord, with the blessing, which is from You, by the coming down upon it of Your Holy Spirit." Here, the priest signs the paten and the chalice together, and the congregation answer, "Amen."

As for sanctifying the sacrifice, according to the *Liturgy of Serapion*, it is through the might and fellowship of the Father.

"Fill this sacrifice" is completed by the coming of the Trinity and His work in it. Thus, the coming of the Father is with the blessing, the coming of the Son is

---

[315] Baumstark, *op. cit.*, 89-90.

through the sacrifice on the altar, and the coming of the Holy Spirit is through His descent upon it. The eucharist is a revelation of the kingdom of God, the presence of the Father, Son, and Holy Spirit on the oblations placed on the altar.

Calling upon the Holy Spirit to sanctify the oblations before the institution (sanctifying the bread and wine) in the *Liturgy of Mark* is an ancient Egyptian trait unparalleled in the *Coptic Liturgies of Basil or Gregory*.

The *invocation* or *epiclesis* means calling by name or calling God's name on an object to sanctify it. According to Irenaeus of Lyons (130-200) we know that calling by name is a sanctifying process:

> The bread, which is produced from the earth, when it receives the invocation of God, is no longer common bread, but the Eucharist.[316]

The *Liturgy of Mark* is not alone in mentioning this invocation. The same is found in the *Liturgy of James the Brother of the Lord* (before it evolved).[317] Cyril of Jerusalem (315-386) mentioned that the invocation comes immediately after the Sanctus:

> Then having sanctified ourselves by these spiritual Hymns [the Sanctus], we beseech the merciful God to send forth His Holy Spirit.[318]

---

[316] *Against Heresies*, 4.18.5
[317] Brightman, *op. cit.*, 86-88.
[318] NPNF2-7, 294 (*Catechetical Letters: On the Mysteries* V).

This expression mentioned puzzled many liturgists like Gregory Dix (1901-1952) who thinks that Cyril does not refer to a chronological order of the liturgy that he was explaining. Gregory Dix elaborated to prove that Cyril of Jerusalem meant that the invocation of the Holy Spirit came immediately after the Sanctus in the Jerusalem Church rite during the second half of the fourth century.[319]

Mark the Apostle was not alone in referring to the invocation at this early point during the liturgy, before the institution. Serapion of Thmuis also says,

> **Fill** also this sacrifice with Your might and fellowship, because we have offered this living sacrifice, a bloodless sacrifice.

Sacrifice is equivalent to *offering* in this context. The *Bloodless sacrifice* is a phrase used since the fourth century in the writings of the fathers, first used by Cyril of Jerusalem (315-386).[320] In the *Liturgy of Serapion*, this expression means offering a Eucharist, specifically for the bread and wine, which were sanctified in the previous prayers.

The mentioning of the *bloodless sacrifice* before the words of institution is a trait that distinguishes some eucharistic prayers in the Church of Egypt from others.[321]

---

[319] Dix, *op. cit.*, 197-213.
[320] Dix, *op. cit.*, 166.
[321] *Ibid.*

Not only that, but there is also the *living sacrifice* at this juncture of the Eucharistic prayer in the *Liturgy of Serapion*. This is a decisive phrase without any warning or camouflage. Gregory Dix (1901-1952) confessed to his confusion in explaining this phrase. When he could not find previous liturgical words in which sanctification occurred to the sacrificial elements, he said,

> It would be a good deal easier to understand if it [the *living sacrifice*] has a connection with the previous petition, 'we beseech Thee make us *living* me.' In this case the 'living sacrifice and unbloody oblation' will have reference to the 'sacrifice of praise' offered in the hymn of the sanctus, and not to the eucharistic offering which follows.[322]

Liturgists could not avoid linking the two phrases in the *Liturgy of Serapion*: "O Lord of Host, **fill** also this sacrifice with Your might and fellowship, because we have offered this living sacrifice, a bloodless sacrifice," and the words of institution which immediately follow, "To you we *have offered* this bread like the body of Your only-begotten Son. This bread is like the holy body…" The phrase, *have offered*, comes in the past tense, referring to a previous offering of the oblations. As for the *Liturgy of Hippolytus*, it fully separated between what comes before the institution and what comes after, in describing the elements of the holy sacrifice.[323]

Here we see that the entire *Liturgy of Serapion*, titled from its beginning as *Prayer of Offering*, is essentially a Eucharistic prayer fully united with the

---

[322] *Ibid.*
[323] Dix, *op. cit.*, 167.

offertory that precedes it in the offering of the Lamb. Thus, Serapion says, "We have offered..." before the offertory prayers begin.[324]

This very ancient invocation, preserved in the *Liturgy of Mark and Serapion*, before uttering the sanctification on the bread and wine, was not the first invocation. This attracted the attention of liturgists, who devoted to it an unbelievable amount of research. Rather, it was preceded by another invocation to the Person of the Son the Logos in the rite of offering the Lamb, when the priest says in the inaudible prayer of offering the bread and chalice to the Son:

> O Master, Lord Jesus Christ... we ask and entreat Your goodness, O Lover of Mankind, show Your face upon this bread, and upon this cup, which we have set upon this, Your priestly table. Bless them, sanctify them, purify them and change them, in order that, on the one hand, this bread may indeed become Your holy Body, and, on the other hand, the mixture which is in this cup indeed Your precious Blood...[325]

Here it becomes clear that the utterance of the invocation which comes immediately after the Sanctus was with full awareness of the previous invocation in the offering of the lamb, especially in the words of the *Liturgy of Mark*, "Your precious gifts which have been set forth before You..."[326] Subsequently, in this invocation there in not a request to make the bread, the body of Christ, or the wine His blood, but only a request to fill the sacrifice with blessing, completing the sacrifice

---

[324] *Ibid.*
[325] H G Bishop Serapion, and H G Bishop Youssef., *op. cit.*, 122-123.
[326] *Ibid.*, 386.

with blessing from the Father, and sanctifying it by the descent upon it by the Holy Spirit.

Therefore, the first invocation (in the rite of offering the Lamb) is directed to the Person of the Son, but this invocation, which comes before the sanctification on the bread and wine, is to the Person of the Holy Spirit. Yet, when the liturgies developed in the fourth century, the focus was on the invocation of the Holy Spirit which occurs after the sanctification of the bread and wine to change them into the precious Body and Blood of Christ. With the intense focus on this invocation, the significance of the former invocations diminished.[327]

---

[327] In the *Liturgy of Serapion*, the offertory simply consists of the deacon offering the oblations on the altar.

Priest: And blessed.

Congregation: Amen.

Priest: And sanctified.

Congregation: Amen.

Priest: And broke and gave it to His holy disciples and apostles saying, 'Take eat this is My body, which for your sake and for any is broken and distributed (κλώμενον καὶ διαδιδόμενον) for the remission of sins. Do this in remembrance of Me. And likewise also the chalice after they ate, He mixed it of wine and water and thanked.

Congregation: Amen.

Priest: And blessed.

Congregation: Amen.

Priest: And sanctified.

Congregation: Amen.

Priest: And He tasted and gave it also to His holy disciples and apostles saying, 'Take, drink of it all of you. This is my blood which is for the new covenant, which is shed for you and for many, for the remission of sins. Do this in remembrance of Me. For each time you eat this bread and drink this cup, you preach My death, and confess My resurrection and ascension (καὶ ἀνάληψιν) until I come.

The Oldest Greek Institution Narrative in the Liturgy of Gregory

The oldest Greek *Institution Narrative* in the *Liturgy of Gregory* is found in the BnF Manuscript No. 325 (Greeks) and the F. Kacmarcik Codex. It says,

Priest: I offer You, O my Master, the symbols of my freedom. I write my works according to Your sayings. You are He who has given me (this service),[331] full of mystery. You have given me the partaking of Your Flesh, in bread and wine.

Congregation: We believe.

Priest: For in the same night in which You gave Yourself up of Your own will and authority alone, You took bread into Your holy hands, which are without spot or blemish, blessed, and life-giving. You looked up towards heaven to God, who is Your Father and Master of everyone. And when You had given thanks, You blessed it, You sanctified it. You broke it and gave it to Your own holy, honorable disciples and saintly apostles, saying, "Take, eat of it, all of you. For this is My Body, which is broken for you and for many, to be given for the remission of sins. This do in remembrance of Me." Likewise also, after they had supped, You took a cup and mixed it of the fruit of the vine and water. And when You had given thanks, You blessed it, You sanctified it. You tasted and gave it also to Your own holy, honorable disciples and saintly apostles, saying, "Take, drink of it, all of you. For this is My Blood of the New Covenant, which is shed for you and for many, to be given for the remission of sins. This do in remembrance of Me." "For every time you eat of this bread and drink of this cup, you proclaim My Death, confess My Resurrection (and ascension), and remember Me till I come."

The Oldest Greek Institution Narrative in the Liturgy of Mark

The oldest Greek *Institution Narrative* in the *Liturgy of Mark* is found in the Balayza Monastery

---

[331] Words in parenthesis are the corrections by W. F. Macomber to the Greek based on the F. Kacmarcik Codex.

manuscript dating to the sixth century, which was discovered near Assiut in 1907:

> For our Lord Jesus Christ, on the night in which He was given up, took bread on His holy hands, gave thanks, blessed it, sanctified it, divided it, and gave it to His disciples and apostles, saying: Take, eat of it, all of you. This is my body, which is given for you for the remission of sins.
>
> And so also after supper he took the cup, blessed and drank from it, and gave it to them, saying: Take and drink from it, all of you. This is my blood shed for you for the remission of sins. Every time you eat of this bread and drink of this cup, announcing my death, acknowledging my resurrection, you remember me.

The *Institution Narrative* in the *Liturgy of Serapion*

The *Institution Narrative* in the *Liturgy of Serapion* exhibits the distinct features pertaining to the Egyptian liturgy:

> To thee we **have offered** this bread the likeness of the body of the only-begotten. This bread is the likeness of the holy body, because the Lord Jesus Christ in the night in which he was betrayed took bread and broke and gave to his disciples saying, "Take ye and eat, this is my body which is being broken for you for remission of sins." Wherefore we also making the likeness of the death **have offered** the bread, and beseech thee through this sacrifice, be reconciled to all of us and be merciful, God of truth...[332] We

---

[332] The following is inserted in the *Liturgy of Serapion*: "and as this bread had been scattered on the top of the mountains and gathered together came to be one, so also gather thy holy Church out of every nation and every country and every city and village and house and make one living catholic church." Gregory Dix sees that this segment interrupts the flow of the words of institution. Likewise,

have offered also the cup, the likeness of the blood, because the Lord Jesus Christ, taking a cup after supper, said to his own disciples, "Take ye, drink, this is the new covenant, which is my blood, which is being shed for you for remission of sins." Wherefore we **have also offered** the cup, presenting [it] a likeness of the blood.[333]

An Explanation for the Institution Narrative

All Eastern Liturgies, relying on the words of Paul the Apostle in his Epistle to the Corinthians,[334] narrate what the Lord instituted on the night He gave Himself up to suffer for our sins. In the Eastern tradition, the ecclesiastical day begins with sunset and ends in the following sunset. In the Western tradition, the liturgy mentions that the Lord instituted the mystery on the day before His Passion, because the Latin Church counts the day from midnight to midnight.[335]

The *Liturgy of Serapion* (along with all Coptic Liturgies) links the first phrase of offering the elements of the sacrifice with the words of the institutive narrative. All the liturgies mention, "He took bread on His hands..." after the introduction to the institution, which comes as one expression or a short connector. The

---

describing wheat, of which the Eucharistic bread is made, as scattered on the tops of the mountains does not agree with the flat nature of the Nile Valley, which means that this expression is not a product of this local prayer originating in Thmuis near the Nile Delta. Actually, this is taken from the prayer found in the ninth chapter of the *Didache*. Therefore, this segment is not of the origin of the *Liturgy of Serapion*. Cf. Dix, *op. cit.*, 167.

[333] Wordsworth, *op. cit.*, 62-63.
[334] 1 Corinthians 11.23
[335] Ignatius Aphraim, *op. cit.*, 274.

Liturgy of Gregory deviates from this standard somewhat as this link is slightly prolonged.

In the *Liturgy of Mark*, this connection is, "For our Lord Jesus Christ in the night in which He gave Himself up," which was expanded thereafter to become, "For Your only-begotten Son, our Lord, God, Savior, and King of us all, Jesus Christ, in the night in which He was about to give Himself up to suffer for our sins, and the death, which He accepted by His own will for us all."

In the *Liturgy of Serapion*, this connection is, "Because the Lord Jesus Christ in the night in which he was betrayed." Notice dear reader that the linker in the *Liturgy of Mark* exactly matches that of the *Liturgy of Serapion*.[336]

In the *Liturgy of Basil*, the connection is:

> He instituted for us this great Mystery of godliness. For being determined to give Himself up to death for the life of the world.[337]

The distinct feature of the Alexandrine liturgy (which is mainly exclusive to the *Liturgies of Mark and Serapion*) is the narration of the *Institution Narrative* in the past tense.

The *Liturgy of Serapion* stipulates that the actual offering of the oblations had occurred in the offertory, the rite of offering the Lamb. Hence, the *Institution Narrative* comes in the past tense, saying, "**have offered**,"

---

[336] Wordsworth, *op. cit.*, 62.
[337] H G Bishop Serapion, and H G Bishop Youssef., *op. cit.*, 189-190.

to confirm an offering that occurred in the past. It says, "We **have offered** also the cup, the likeness of the blood," and, "Wherefore we also making the likeness of the death **have offered** the bread," and, "To thee we **have offered** this bread the likeness of the body of the only-begotten." As for the *Liturgy of Mark*, the *Institution Narrative* is immediately preceded by, "Your precious gifts which **are already set forth before You**, this bread and this cup..."[338] This is not indicated in the *Liturgy of Hippolytus*.

Gregory Dix (1901-1952), with a Western scholarly viewpoint, says that the *Institution Narrative* is the pivot of all Eucharistic prayers, and the justifier of all the church's actions during the Eucharist.[339] Meanwhile, the East (in contrast) focused on the invocation of the Holy Spirit towards the end of the liturgy, as the pivot and the climax of the Eucharist.

Western theology artificially sheds light on *important elements*, and extracts from the liturgical prayers the *important moments*. In the eucharist, there is the *moment* of transforming the oblations, which occurs in the institution narrative, and thereafter the communion. In baptism, it is the *moment* of triple immersion. In weddings, it is the *pronouncing*. However, we cannot separate between the *importance* of these moments and the greater liturgical framework, which alone can reveal its genuineness. From here, we touch upon the gaps that tarnish the Western theological explanations of the mysteries.

---

[338] H G Bishop Serapion, and H G Bishop Youssef., *op. cit.*, 377.
[339] Dix, *op. cit.*, 167.

The Rites Accompanying the Institution Narrative

In the *Liturgy of Basil*, the priest begins the *Institution Narrative* by saying, "He left us this great Mystery…" or its equivalent in the other liturgies.

The Ritual Practice over the Bread

Ibn Sebā' says,

> The priest say, 'He left us this great mystery.' And at saying this, he nods to the oblation in the paten, before censing his hands over the censer, then he places his hands on the censor, turning it thrice in count with the Holy Trinity, then he moves to the paten, removing the cloth which is under the oblation, and says, 'He took bread on His pure hands, and lifted His eyes to heaven saying.' At this point he lifts up the oblation onto his hands and says as Christ said, 'Take, eat, this is my Body, which is sacrificed for you for the remission of sins,' and the congregation say, 'We believe, we confess, we glorify'…[340]

This simple rite was expanded somewhat by Pope Gabriāl V (1409-1427) and additionally with Hegumen 'Abd al-Massīh Salīb al-Mass'ūdī al-Baramūsī (1848-1935). If the basis is one for all, the rites varied from one place to another, and from time to time.

Pope Gabriāl V places the priest's censing his hands three times over the censor at an earlier, before saying, "He instituted for us this great mystery…" Upon this utterance, he does not nod his head to the oblations, but points with his hands to the bread and wine placed

---

[340] Yohanna Ibn A'bī Zakaria Ibn Sebā', *op. cit.*, 249.

before him. Then, when he lifts up the cloth from the paten, after taking the oblation onto his hands, he kisses the cloth and places it on his eyes, then he explains the first stage of the fractioning the oblation (something Ibn Sebā' does not mention).

Here Pope Gabriāl V says:

> The serving deacon offers the censer to the serving priest, who censes his hands the censer trice, to prepare to touch that which is placed before him and carry it on his hands. At saying, "He instituted for us this great mystery of godliness,"[341] he points with his hands to the bread and wine placed before him. And when he says, "He took bread,"[342] he takes the oblation onto his hands, lifts the cloth that is in the paten, kisses it, places it on his eyes, and laves it on the altar. Saying, "He looked up to heaven,"[343] he looks up to heaven. Saying, "and He blessed,"[344] he signs the oblation once, continues, "and He blessed,"[345] and signs the oblation once, and continues, "and He sanctified,"[346] and he signs the oblation once. They are a total of three signings.
>
> Saying, "And He broke,"[347] he fractions the oblation into two-thirds and one-third gently without separating them from each other, and without touching the Despotikon, rather he is very careful lest any piece of it chip away. Saying, "Who breaks,"[348] he gently empties the top of the oblation, without breaking it, and places it in the patent,

---

[341] Pope Gabriel V mentioned this phrase in Coptic, only.
[342] *Ibid.*
[343] *Ibid.*
[344] *Ibid.*
[345] *Ibid.*
[346] *Ibid.*
[347] *Ibid.*
[348] *Ibid.*

and cleans his hands inside the patent lest any of the oblation adheres to them.

In Euchologion (1902), Hegumen ʿAbd al-Massīh Salīb al-Massʿūdī al-Baramūsī (1848-1935) mentions that at the beginning of the *Institution Narrative* that the priest points with his hands to the bread and wine while saying, "He instituted for us this great mystery…," then he censes his hands with the censer. While the priests says the previous phrase, "He instituted for us this great mystery of godliness," he lifts his hands off the censer with incense and says, "For being determined to give Himself up to death for the life of the world." When he takes the oblation onto his hands, he lifts up the cloth under it on the patent, kisses it, and then he adds, "The priest places his right hand on the bread which is in his left hand, and looks up saying, "And He looked up to heaven…" At the signings, he mentions that the priest signs the bread with his fingers.

When he comes to the first stage of fractioning, Hegumen ʿAbd al-Massīh Salīb al-Massʿūdī al-Baramūsī mentions that it is to be by his right thumb, not with his nail, having his fingernails clipped lest anything clings to them (here or during communion), fractioning from top to bottom.[349] The rest of the instructions, he takes verbatim from Pope Gabriāl V.

It becomes clear that the Euchologion (1902) was describing what was not fully written in our ancient ritual books, besides mentioning certain parts and not others.

---

[349] *Euchologion (1902)*, 331.

In the *Liturgy of Basil*, the priest censes his hands while saying,

> He instituted for us this great Mystery of godliness. For being determined to give Himself up to death for the life of the world.[350]

In the *Liturgy of Gregory*, the priest censes his hands while saying,

> For in the same night in which You gave Yourself up of Your own will and authority alone.

In the *Liturgy of Cyril*, the priest censes his hands while saying,

> In the night in which He was about to give Himself up to suffer for our sins — and the death, which He accepted by His own will for us all.

Before he censes his hands over the censer, the priest signs the incense box and places one spoonful into the censer. This spoonful comes in the *Liturgy of Basil* a little earlier, as the priest says, "He incarnated and took flesh..." Although the ritual instructions point in the *Liturgies of Gregory and Cyril* to signing the incense box once before placing a spoonful into the censer at this time, the ritual instructions for the *Liturgy of Basil* do not mention this.

Ibn Sebā' was very precise in describing the priest's censing his hands over the censer three times, mentioning that after censing them, he moves them to

---

[350] H G Bishop Serapion, and H G Bishop Youssef., *op. cit.*, 189-190.

the paten to the oblations. Pope Gabriāl V sufficed to say that the priest censing his hands is in preparation to handling the holy oblation. This explanation takes away from the significance of this ritual practice, because purifying the hands is the base reason. The intended meaning for this practice is that the incense that the priest transfers from the censer to the oblations placed on the altar proclaims that the Sacrifice on the altar is Himself Christ of Glory, who offered Himself up on the cross for the salvation of our race. The good Father smelt Him as an aroma of delight and acceptance for the salvation of the world. Also, the priest censes his hands three times over the censer (or turning them three times according to Ibn Sebā') because the Holy Trinity participated in the work of redemption, which was fulfilled by the incarnation, crucifixion, and resurrection of the Second Person.

Hegumen 'Abd al-Massīh Salīb al-Mass'ūdī al-Baramūsī was precise while documenting the oral tradition handed down to us from generation to generation. He mentions that the priest,

> ... takes the bread onto his hands... the priest places his right hand over the bread which is on his left hand, and look up saying, "And He looked up..."

Here, it becomes clear that the priest, when he carries the bread on his hands, with both hands, he returns it from his right hand to his left hand. This is a ritual stemming from the Old Testament. It is worth noting that all Coptic liturgies and most liturgies, East and West, mention that, "Took bread on his Hands," in the plural sense. Even the Byzantine Liturgy of John

Chrysostom says, "He took bread with His hands." The Greek text of the *Coptic Liturgy of Gregory* mentions, "He took bread in His hands (ἐν ταῖς ... σου χερσὶν)."

When the priest initiates the *Institution Narrative*, the deacons in the altar light candles, which they carry in their hands. Hence, the narration of the passion, crucifixion, and death ultimately led to the light of resurrection from the dead, giving light to life. The lit candle at the altar, during the Eucharistic prayer is symbolic of Christ's resurrection, which scattered the darkness of death and gave light to life and eternity.[351]

Ritual Practice on the Chalice

Ibn Sebā' writes:

> Then the priest picks up the chalice with his hands and says, "And also the cup after supper, He mixed of wine and water, saying, 'Drink of this all of you. This is My blood for the New Covenant which is shed for you all for the remission of sins,'" and as he says *shed*, he tilts the chalice to the right, a sign of shedding (not shaking it like other priests). And the congregation say, "Again we believe, confess, and glorify," as before.

Pope Gabriāl V writes:

> Saying, "And the cup also,"[352] he holds the chalice with his finger until he repeats as before. He signs the chalice

---

[351] Here I repeat that the use of electric candles on the altar loses the significance behind the use of candles and its spiritual meaning. The sanctuary or the church should be lit by candles and oil lanterns.

[352] Pope Gabriel V mentioned this phrase in Coptic, only.

three times: signing "He thanked,"[353] signing "He blessed,"[354] signing "He sanctified,"[355] for a total of three signings.

After the signings, he holds it with his hand until he says, "Take, drink of it all of you,"[356] when he tilts the chalice gently in the form of the cross without disturbing it. Saying, "For this is my blood,"[357] he points with his hands to the chalice also. Then, saying, "For every time you eat of this bread,"[358] he points to the bread, and when he says, "And drink of this cup," he points with his hands to the chalice..."[359]

The Euchologion (1902) writes:

The priest places his hand on the tip of the chalice saying, "And also the cup..." The priest holds the mouth of the chalice with his hand saying, "And tasted and gave also to His disciples..." He moves the chalice in the form of the cross, gently tilting without disturbing it, first towards the West, then East, north, and south, while saying, "Take drink of it all of you." Next, he points with his hands to the chalice saying, "For this is My blood which is for the New Covenant..."

The *Church Order* Manuscript No. 118 (Rites) in the patriarchate in Cairo from 1911, after mentioning the three signings on the chalice as the priest says, "He thanked, blessed, and sanctified," adds:

---

[353] *Ibid.*
[354] *Ibid.*
[355] *Ibid.*
[356] *Ibid.*
[357] *Ibid.*
[358] *Ibid.*
[359] Pope Gabriel V mentioned this phrase in Coptic, only.

He holds the chalice and says, "ⲁϥϫⲉⲙϯⲡⲓ (He tasted)." When he says, "Ϫⲉ ⲃⲓ ⲥⲱ (Take drink)," he tilts the chalice to the four directions in the form of the cross with gentle agility without upset. Next, he points with the chalice a half circle from right to left (without going any further), and restores the chalice to its place. The warning against circuiting twice or trice is fear lest any spill from it…"

The ritual practices differed beginning at the words of institution on the chalice: Ibn Sebāʿ says that the priest carries the chalice in his hands, Pope Gabriāl V says that the priest holds the chalice with his fingers, while Hegumen ʿAbd al-Massīh Salīb al-Massʿūdī al-Baramūsī says that the priest places his hand on the tip of the chalice.

Not only this, but we find another ritual indicator coming from the twelfth century, which is observed by all Coptic churches until this day. Although it is the only indicator which was not documented in the ritual books, it is mentioned in *Wisdom of the Egyptian Fathers* where it says,

> The priest places his hand on the tip of the chalice, circuiting its rim with his finger, because the blood of the covenant was sprinkled in around the Mercy seat, though it is now not poured out but is given for sinners to gain life.[360]

During the words of the institution over the chalice, the ritual practices have also differed: Ibn Sebāʿ writes that when the priest says, *shed*, he tilts the chalice to the right, as sign of shedding His blood, not shaking it as do many priests. Pope Gabriāl V moved the tilting

---

[360] Presbyter Samʿān Ibn Kalīl, *op. cit.*, 88.

of the chalice a little earlier than what is mentioned by Ibn Sebāʿ: the priest tilting the chalice, not only to the right but in all four directions in the form of a cross, says, "Take, drink of it all of you." This rite is also mentioned by the *Church Order* Manuscript No. 118 (Rites) in the patriarchate in Cairo from 1911, with a slight difference.

These diverse practices are variations in the expression of the main ritual belief. What is noticeable is that the ancient ritual practices were generally simple, and not long or complex.

Moving the chalice in this moment is equivalent to offering it before the Lord, exactly as the priest offered the bread in his hands. It is a ritualistic movement preserved by the Coptic Church.

Development in the Institution Narrative

The words of the institution vary from one liturgy to another, yet the main expressions remained the same in all the liturgies. While the *Coptic Liturgy of Basil* says,

> ...For being determined to give Himself up to death for the life of the world,

The *Syriac Liturgy of James the Brother of the Lord*, says,

> And when he was about to accept a voluntary death for us sinners, himself without sin.[361]

---

[361] Brightman, *op. cit.*, 86.

He took Bread

All liturgies, East and West, contain the phrase, "He took bread," being the very ancient abbreviated phrase which does not mention the additions of "on His hands," or, "with His hands," or any reference to Christ's divine hands.

In the oldest Sahidic-Coptic manuscript of the *Liturgy of Basil*, the Doresse manuscript, which dates to the fourth century, the priest says, "He took bread, blessed it, sanctified it, broke it..." We find an even shorter segment in the *Liturgy of Hippolytus* from the beginnings of the third century: "He took bread, and thanked..." We find this same short phrase in the *Liturgy of Serapion*, "[He] took bread and broke and gave to his disciples saying, 'Take ye and eat.'"[362] Likewise in the Syriac liturgy of the *Lord's Covenant*, the priest says, "He took bread, gave it to His disciples saying, 'Take, eat, this is my Body.'"

We find the first mention of this divine hand in the Epistle of Clement of Rome to the Corinthians from the end of the first century, although it is an epistle not pointing to a specific liturgical text:

> Above all, with His holy and undefiled hands He formed man... the express likeness of His own image.[363]

The divine hands are characterized as *holy*. This is what we find in the *Liturgy of Mark* in the Balayza

---

[362] Wordsworth, *op. cit.*, 62.
[363] The Apostolic Fathers with Justin Martyr and Irenaeus, 23 (Chapter 33).

Monastery manuscript (sixth century), and likewise in the *Syriac Liturgy of James the Brother of the Lord*.[364]

The *Apostles Constitutions* of the Syrian rite, which scholars date to about 260, added another attribute to the hands,

> He took bread on His holy spotless hands.
> (8.12.36)

Thus, the liturgies borrowed from each other the attributes of those divine hands, until the Coptic liturgy settled on three attributes: "Holy without spot or blemish, blessed, and life-giving." According to the F. Kacmarcik Codex, which has the Greek text for the three Coptic Liturgies, the attribute of *"life-giving,"* was unknown in the *Liturgies of Basil and Gregory* until the fourteenth century. The first mention of this attribute was in the Greek text of the *Coptic Liturgy of Mark*, retrieved from the Greek text to the *Liturgy of James the Brother of the Lord*. Describing the divine hands as *life-giving* is found in Serapion's Euchologion from the fourth century, in the *Prayer of Laying on the Hands on the Catechumens*:

> We stretch out the hand, O Master, and pray that the divine and **living** hand may be stretched out in blessing on this people.[365]

There are other attributes regarding the divine hands found in the Euchologion of Serapion (outside the

---

[364] Brightman, *op. cit.*, 87.
[365] Wordsworth, *op. cit.*, 92.

Eucharistic prayer). We can read them in the *Prayer of Laying on the Hands on the Laity*,

> May the living and clean hand, the hand of the only-begotten, that hath destroyed all evil things and confirmed and established all holy things, be stretched out over the heads of this people.[366]

Below, we will find the attributes of those divine hands from the Greek text of the three Coptic liturgies.

The Greek text of the *Coptic Liturgy of Basil* according to the F. Kacmarcik Codex says:

> He took bread on His holy hands which are without spot and blessed.

This exactly matches the Greek text of the *Liturgy of Basil* published by E. Renaudot in *Patrologia Graeca* (*PG.*, 31), based on BnF Manuscript No. 325 (Greek).

The Greek text of the *Coptic Liturgy of Gregory*, as published by E. Renaudot[367] and the scholar W. F. Macomber, is:

> You took bread in Your holy hands which are without spot or blemish (ἀχράντοις).[368]

The Greek text of the *Liturgy of Cyril* according to the F. Kacmarcik Codex is:

---

[366] *Ibid.*, 92-93.
[367] *PG*, 36.
[368] This Greek word can also mean *absolutely pure*.

He took bread on His holy hands, which are without blemish (ἀχράντων) or spot, blessed, life-giving (ζωοποιῶν).[369]

He looked up

The *Coptic Liturgy of Basil*, as found in the Doresse manuscript (fourth century), the *Liturgy of Serapion* (fourth century), the *Liturgy of Basil* in the Balayza Monastery manuscript (sixth century), the Litrugy of the Apostolic Tradition (third century), the Liturgy of the Lord's Covenant (fifth century), and the Byzantine Liturgy of John Chrysostom do not have, "And He looked up."

The *Apostolic Constitutions* (second half of the fourth century) mentions,

> He looked up, to You His God and Father. (8.12.36)

The Greek text of the *Coptic Liturgy of Basil* according to the F. Kacmarcik Codex mentions, "He looked up to the highest heaven, to You His Father and our God (Θεὸν ἡμῶν), and God of all (καὶ Θεὸν ὅλων)." This is also what is mentioned in the *Liturgy of Gregory* in the same manuscript, "And You looked up to Your Father, our God, and God of all." In the *Liturgy of Mark*, it mentions:

---

[369] Macomber, W.F., *The Anaphora of Saint Mark according to the Kacmarcik codex, op. cit.*, 94.

And He looked to heaven, to You, Your own Father (τὸν ἴδιον Πατέρα), our God and the God of all.[370]

The contemporary text of the Coptic liturgies, "He looked up towards heaven to You, O God, who are His Father and Master of everyone,"[371] is rendered in the third person in the *Liturgies of Basil and Cyril*, and in the second person in the *Liturgy of Gregory*.

In the Byzantine rite, while the *Liturgy of John Chrysostom* is void of this phrase, the *Liturgy of Basil* describes this looking up, "Upward to You O God the Father," retrieving this phrase from the *Liturgy of James the Brother of the Lord*.[372]

When the priest says, "He looked up," he looks up.[373] Meanwhile, the Euchologion (1902) mentions (as we have already stated) that,

> The priest places his right hand on the bread which is on his left hand, and looks up.[374]

He Gave thanks, Blessed, and Sanctified

In the Coptic rite, when the priest signs the oblations with the three signings accompanying these three words, the congregation respond with "Amen."

---

[370] Macomber, W.F., *The Anaphora of Saint Mark according to the Kacmarcik codex, op. cit.*, 94.
[371] H G Bishop Serapion, and H G Bishop Youssef., *op. cit.*, 190, 378.
[372] Brightman, *op. cit.*, 87. "He showed it to thee, God the Father."
[373] Pope Gabriāl V, *op. cit.*, 78.
[374] *Euchologion (1902)*, 331.

This is no the case, however, in the Syriac rite. When the priest says, "...and He thanked, blessed, sanctified, broke, and gave to His holy disciples saying, 'Take, eat of it. This is My body which is sacrificed for you and for many for the remission of sins. Do this in remembrance of my,'" **the deacons and believers respond with "Amen."**

This is also what we find in the Byzantine rite, which does not know these three responses, sufficing with **the chorus answering,** "Amen," after the priest has said,

> ... and He thanked, blessed, sanctified, broke, and gave to His holy apostolic disciples saying, 'Take, eat of it. This is My body which is broken for you for the remission of sins.'

This is the standard for the *Coptic Liturgy of Gregory* in the critical Greek text by E. Renaudot and W. F. Macomber; this is not according to the Coptic rite, but the Syriac.

The Coptic rite excels all other Eastern rites in paying special attention to the congregation's responses and their connection with the priest's prayer, unlike the Roman rite which refused for a long time the participation of any member of the congregation in the liturgical prayers. With time, the Roman rite turned into a rite reserved for the clergy.[375]

---

[375] In the twentieth century, a great movement occurred in the Catholic Church called the *Liturgical Movement*. This movement is closely connected with the ecumenical movement which stemmed from the Catholic Church of Rome in the nineteenth century and continued until now to an even greater extent. Its purpose is to

The three responses of the "Amen" to the three signings in the Coptic rite are responses for the congregation and not the deacons. The congregation, in the Coptic rite, are the ones who confirm the prayer of the priest, not the deacon. Rather, all the responses of the Divine Liturgy are responses for the congregation, not the chorus. Unfortunately, many Eastern rites, especially the Byzantine rite, emphasized the role of the chorus at the cost of the congregation's participation.

The role of the chorus in church is to chant the long hymns for the various ecclesial occasions, but the responses of the Divine Liturgy are the congregation's alone, led by the chorus. All our ritual books (even recent ones) only mention the priest, deacon (or altar deacons), and the congregation. The chorus is not a replacement for the people, but an active assistant to provide the full opportunity for full congregation participation. The ecclesiastic liturgy in its essence is a spiritual concord between the priest and all the congregation in the presence of Christ.

The anaphoras, in this regard, divided into two. One type of anaphoras adhered to the old Hebrew rite

---

convince Christians that worship is not reserved for those who are consecrated in the church, but is the duty of all, clergy and laity equally. This great truth was often forgotten, since the services in the Catholic Church of Rome were in Latin, which prevented the people from full participation. Also, the forms set for prayer in the other Christian denominations were left for the priest or servant to read them, not giving the laity a chance to participate in common worship. This *Liturgical Movement* produced fruit, changing much, such that worship has become a joint work of the whole church.

in which the blessing is the blessing of God the Father on the bread, who did not bless on the bread itself as in "and He blessed it," but rather, "and He blessed," that is, God the Father blessed on it.

This is what we find in the all the Coptic Liturgies in their Greek text, where we find the response, "Amen," following the priest's words (in the *Liturgies of Basil and Mark*): "Thanked (εὐχαριστήσας)," "Blessed (Εὐλογήσας)," and, "Sanctified (Ἁγιάσας)," whether in sanctifying the bread or the chalice.[376]

What confirms the Coptic anaphora's awareness that the blessing, or the verbs of sanctification, are directed to God the Father, not the bread and chalice, is mentioned in the Greek text of the *Coptic Liturgy of Gregory*, "You thanked, and blessed, and sanctified (ηὐχαρίστησας, ηὐλόγησας, ἡγίασας)," whether on the bread or the chalice.[377]

The second type of anaphoras freed itself of this old Hebrew articulation, saying, "He blessed it" "sanctified it." This expression is what we find in the Coptic text of the three Coptic liturgies. Yet, the verb *thanked* in "He thanked," maintained its old traditional position, since no one can say, "God thanked the Father.:

When the priest says, "He thanked, and blessed, and sanctified," he signs the cross. The cross being offered reveals to us the unseen relationship between

---

[376] Macomber, W.F., *The Anaphora of Saint Mark according to the Kacmarcik codex, op. cit.*, 95.
[377] *PG*, 31, 1637.

the Father and His Son Jesus Christ, because when He thanked the Father, He offered His life on the cross; words cannot express this ineffable mystery. The church offers the oblation to the Father according to this order and type, thanking the Father by the cross of His Son Jesus Christ. The cross, apart from the words, becomes the seal of thanksgiving and praise.

Some people in Upper Egypt sign themselves by the cross, when the priest says the words to sanctify the bread and wine, because out of their piety they consider themselves one with the Lord, being baptized and having confessed His death, and were buried with Him in baptism. They offer themselves through the sign of the cross, an acceptable living sacrifice.[378]

Amen typically translates into *so be it,* although its meaning is much stronger. *Amen* does not simply mean *agreement,* but further means *active acceptance,* to be defined as, "Yes, indeed, so be it." It is an expression that concludes every prayer by the serving servant.

Augustine of Hippo says,

> Say 'Amen' over your condition. Seal this by your response. You hear, "the Body of Christ," and you answer, "Amen." May He fulfil your wishes, your participation it he body of Christ... let the mysteries be a place to practice your truths...[379]

He broke and gave to His disciples

---

[378] Presbyter Samʿān Ibn Kalīl, *op. cit.,* 86-87.
[379] *PG,* 38, 1247.

The Liturgy of the *Apostolic Tradition* of Hippolytus agrees with the Clementine Liturgy in Book VIII of the *Apostolic Constitutions*, and the *Liturgy of Serapion*, on, "Gave His disciples," while the Balayza monastery papyrus adds, "and apostles." Meanwhile, the *Liturgy of Basil* according to the Doresse manuscript says, "His holy disciples and His apostles."

In the *Greek Liturgy of Basil*,

He broke it and gave it to His holy disciples and apostles.

In the *Greek Liturgy of Gregory*,

You broke and gave to Your disciples and holy apostles.

In the *Greek Liturgy of Cyril*,

He broke it and gave it to His disciples and saintly blessed apostles.

Κλάσας διέδωκε τοῖς ἁγιός καὶ μακαρίοις αὐτοῦ μαθηταῖς καὶ ἀποστόλοις.

The chain of attributes describing the disciplines began in the *Liturgy of James the Brother of the Lord*, and from there spread to the other rites.

Take eat this is my body... take drink this is my blood

The ancient liturgies all have this phrase, which is extreme in its simplicity. However, it was further modified to become, "Take eat **of it all of you**... take drink **of it all of you**."

The *Liturgy of the Apostolic Tradition* of Hippolytus, along with the *Liturgy of Serapion*, in agreement with the *Apostolic Constitutions*, and the ancient *Liturgy of James the Brother of the Lord* do not have, "of it all of you."

The first addition to this simple phrase was, "**of it**," becoming, "Take eat **of it**." This is what we find in the *Syriac Liturgy of James the Brother of the Lord*, in Greek.[380]

The oldest *Liturgy of Basil* in Sahidic-Coptic found in the Doresse manuscript, mentions, "of it all of you." In agreement with this is the Balayza Monastery papyrus, which contains the oldest Greek text known to date of the *Liturgy of Mark*.

The Syriac rite has the phrase, "of it all of you," in reference to drinking the chalice, but not in reference to eating the bread. The Syriac scholar Ibn al-ʿEbrī (1225-1286) comments:

> Because the bread is food for all, no one forbids himself of eating bread. As for wine, the Nazarites, the vowed, and the solitaries prevented themselves from drinking wine. Since wine is the mystery of the blood of redemption, therefore He ordered the disciples and all believers in His name to drink wine dutifully in partaking of the holy oblation in both forms.

Ephrem the Syrian (306-373) says,

> He called the bread his living body, and filled it personally with the spirit… take, eat with faith, do not doubt anyone

---

[380] Brightman, *op. cit.*, 87.

that it is my body. And that all who eat of it with faith eats fire and spirit. Eat of it all of you, eat in it the holy spirit, because it is my body indeed.

The Lord of glory desired our unity with Him to be on the physical level of eating and drinking, so that we become, as Paul the Apostle said, flesh of His flesh and bones of His bones by an indescribable mystery. A mystery that we cannot intellectually grasp. The command comes from God: "Take, eat." Shall we not obey?

There is a marvellous inaudible prayer in the Byzantine rite, in which the priest says,

> ... I wish that You would give us by Your own honorable hand, Your pure Body and precious Blood, and through us to all the people.

Concerning this, Ambrose of Milan (339-397) says,

> Christ Himself declares, through the priest, 'This is My body.'

By this the Lord confirms that the Eucharist is a sacrifice. As for the demonstrative pronoun, "this," it is specific to the bread and wine, not to the body and blood. Christ here is holding the bread by means of the priest, and says, "This is My Body," that is, "This bread is My body," and holds the chalice saying, "This is My Blood."

Serapion explains this by saying,

> Wherefore we also making the likeness of the death have offered the bread, and beseech thee through this sacrifice, be reconciled to all of us and be merciful, God of truth... We have offered also the cup, the likeness of the blood.[381]

Paul the Apostle made this clear by saying,

> For I received from the Lord that which I also delivered to you: that the Lord Jesus on the same night in which He was betrayed took bread; and when He had given thanks, He broke it and said, "Take, eat; this is My body which is broken for you; do this in remembrance of Me."[382]

The eucharist bread is Christ's divine Body, true Body (ἀλήθεια), and the Eucharistic wine is Christ's true Blood, not in shape and taste. True Body and true Blood, undetectable by the natural physical senses. Otherwise, the mystery would not be a mystery. How can our senses perceive the divinity? Yet, the Holy Spirit declares Him to whom He wishes, in the way He wishes, at the time He wishes. And who is fit for this?

Broken for You and for many... shed for you and for many

In the Balayza monastery papyrus:

> This is my body, sacrificed for you for the remission of sins.

In *Liturgy of Serapion*:

> This is my body, which is broken for you for the remission of sins.

---

[381] Wordsworth, *op. cit.*, 62.
[382] 1 Corinthians 11.23-24

All Coptic liturgies, whether in their Greek or Coptic versions, contain: "for you and for many," or, "for the sake of you and for many."

The phrase, "for you and for many (τὸ ὑπὲρ ὑμῶν καὶ πολλῶν)," means, "every person," the majority that means all.

When the priest says, "The bread which is broken for you and for many," he fractions the bread without parting it. Concerning this, Jacob of Serugh (451-521) says,

> The priest fractions the bread in the shape of the cross, without separating it its parts from each other, because the Lord bears the Passion while He Himself is the Life-giver. He whom death could not overcome, not one of His bones having been broken.

Given for the remission of sins

The *Gospel of John the Evangelist* indicates, *"The bread that I shall give is My flesh, which I shall give for the life of the world."*[383] The only evangelist who said that the blood, according to the utterance of Christ, is for the remission of sins, is Matthew the Evangelist.[384] He did not say this regarding the body because the blood of the Jewish Passover sacrifice was for the atonement of sins, but its flesh was for fellowship. The church repeated, "given for the remission of sins," on the body, as on the blood, considering that it is one sacrifice, and that all

---

[383] John 6.51
[384] Matthew 26.27-28

that is to the blood is to the body, and all that is to the body is to the blood.

As for the Final Confession, while carrying the holy body on his hands, the priest says,

> Given for us for salvation, forgiveness of sins, and eternal life to those who partake of Him.

Do this in remembrance of Me

The Coptic Liturgy is distinct from other liturgical rites in mentioning this phrase twice, firstly after sanctifying the bread, and secondly after sanctifying the blood. Each time the people confirm by, "this is in truth. Amen," considering the bread and the wine as two distinct elements of the holy sacrifice, each separately representing the sacrifice.

The ancient *Syriac Liturgy of James the Brother of the Lord* says, "Do this in remembrance of Me," or, "This do in remembrance of Me," after sanctifying the bread and wine together.

> After sanctifying the bread, when the **priest** says, "...given for the remission of sins," the congregation respond, "Amen."
>
> The **priest** continues, "And likewise also the cup after he had supped when he had mixed with wine and water he gave thanks, blessed, hallowed, and gave to his disciples and holy apostles saying, 'Take, drink ye all of it: this is my blood of the new testament which for you and for many is

shed and given for the remission of sins and for eternal life."[385]

Congregation: Amen.

Priest: Do this in remembrance of Me: for as often as ye eat this bread and drink this cup ye do proclaim my death and confess my resurrection until I come.

Deacons: We believe and confess.

Congregation: Thy death, O Lord, we commemorate and thy resurrection we confess.[386]

The phrase, "This do in remembrance of Me," was accidentally removed from the Byzantine *Liturgy of John Chrysostom*. It is also strange that this phrase is missing in the *Liturgy of Serapion*.

Likewise, the cup after supper, He mixed with wine and water

The *Liturgy of the Apostolic Tradition*, *Liturgy of Serapion*, and the oldest Greek text of the *Liturgy of Mark* in the Balayza Monastery manuscript all agree in not mentioning the mixing of wine and water. Thus, the ancient rite of the Alexandrine Church and the Roman Church do not mention mixing wine with water in the *Institution Narrative*.

However, the *Liturgy of the Apostolic Constitutions*, of the Syriac rite, mentions this phrase clearly:

---

[385] Patriarchal Magazine, Damascus: 1994.
[386] Brightman, *op. cit.*, 87.

> Also the cup, He mixed it of wine and water, sanctified, and gave them saying, 'Drink of it all of you. This is my blood. Which is shed for many for the remission of sins. Do this in remembrance of Me.
> (8.12.37)

This is also what we find in the *Liturgy of James the Brother of the Lord*, preserved in the Syrian Church, where the sanctification of the chalice is,

> Likewise after supper He took the cup and mixed it of wine and water, and looked up to heaven, and showed it to Thee His God and Father, and gave thanks and hallowed and blessed and filled it with holy spirit and gave to His holy and blessed disciples saying...[387]

The focus of the Coptic liturgy, however, turned from mixing the wine and water to the words of the institution. We find in the oldest Sahidic-*Coptic Liturgy of Basil* in the Doresse manuscript:

> Likewise the cup also after the supper, He mixed of wine and water.

Although mixing the wine and water, as a ritual is extremely ancient, yet we cannot determine the time of its entry into the *Institution Narrative*, especially since the Coptic Church mixed the wine and water in the rite of offering the Lamb, without any words accompanying this mixture.

While the Syrians mix the wine and water in an external container before placing them in the chalice, the Byzantine rite mixes the wine and water twice: once at

---

[387] Dix, *op. cit.*, 190.

the beginning of the offering of the Lamb, and another at the end of the liturgy, when the priest says, "The Holies for the holy," at which time they pour warm water into the chalice, after sanctifying the mixed water.

He tasted and gave also to His disciples

Tasted is not mentioned in any of the ancient liturgies. It is not found in the oldest *Greek Liturgy of Mark* in the Balayza Monastery papyrus. Even the oldest Sahidic-*Coptic Liturgy of Basil* (sixth-seventh century) is void of this word, which is indicated by the Doresse manuscript. However, *tasted* pertains to the Alexandrine rite, however it entered the *Institution Narrative* at a somewhat later stage. This term is not found in the anaphoras of the other rites, except the Syriac liturgies like the *Liturgy of Mar Basilious* and the *Liturgy of the Twelve Apostles* that retrieved this term from the Coptic liturgies.

As for the Coptic rite, this word is found in the Greek text of the *Liturgy of Mark*[388] in the F. Kacmarcik Codex from the fourteenth century and in the *Greek Liturgy of Basil* published by E. Renaudot. The word, however, is not found in the Greek text of the *Coptic Liturgy of Gregory*. The *Anaphora of Mark* focused on this term, and from there it was transmitted to the *Coptic Liturgies of Basil and Gregory*.

---

[388] Macomber, W.F., *The Anaphora of Saint Mark according to the Kacmarcik codex, op. cit.*, 95.

The Coptic priest practices what he says at the end of the Divine Liturgy as he first tastes from the chalice before it to the deacons and congregation.[389]

Take Drink

All Alexandrine anaphoras preserve this phrase, "Take drink." The *Liturgy of Serapion* explains to us the ancient Alexandrine rite as it says,

> Take ye, drink, this is the new covenant, which is my blood, which is being shed for you for remission of sins.[390]

The Balayza Monastery manuscript adds to this, "of it all of you," saying,

> Take, drink of it all of you, this is my blood shed for you for the remission of sins.

"My Blood which is for the new covenant" is a later addition in the Eucharistic text as it is not found in the Balayza Monastery manuscript (*Greek Liturgy of Mark*) or the White Monastery manuscript (*Coptic Liturgy of Basil*). It is also unknown in the liturgical tradition of Hippolytus. Perhaps, the *Liturgy of Serapion* is the first from which this phrase stemmed, which says,

> This is the new covenant, which is my blood, which is being shed for you.[391]

---

[389] *Euchologion (1902)*, 414.
[390] Wordsworth, *op. cit.*, 63.
[391] *Ibid.*

The *Liturgy of Serapion* imitated with astonishing precision the Lord's very words as mentioned in the Holy Gospel,

This cup is the new covenant in My blood.[392]

"*My Blood which is for the new covenant*" is found in all the Coptic liturgies, in both the Greek and Coptic texts, from after the sixth or seventh century.

The mystery of the Eucharist cannot be understood without faith. This is the true blood which can sanctify, purify, completely heal, and forgive the sins of all who partake of it. It is not like any Old Testament sacrifice, which was a reminder of the person's sins before God. It is impossible for the blood of bulls and goats to remove sins. The Lord Jesus, after He offered for sins one sacrifice with His blood, sat forever on the righthand of God.[393]

The new covenant with the blood of Jesus became the continual remission of our sins, for all who partake of it.

<u>**For each time you eat... and drink... you proclaim my death and confess my resurrection, and remember me till I come**</u>

The Alexandrine rite continued to mention nothing except the death of the Lord, according to the

---

[392] Luke 22.20
[393] Hebrews 10.1-9

teachings of Paul the Apostle, who says that the commemoration is only of the Lord's death:

> For as often as you eat this bread and drink this cup, you proclaim the Lord's death till He comes.[394]

The tradition continued in effect until the era of liturgical revisions in the fourth century. We notice that the *Liturgy of Basil*, according to the Doresse manuscript (dated by scholars to before the fourth century), preserved this tradition:

> For each time you eat of this bread, and drink of this cup, you confess my death till I come.

From an early time, the resurrection of the Lord was added to most liturgies; however, this was after mentioning His death, according to the words of Paul the Apostle.

Although the Greek text of all the Coptic liturgies mentions, "And confess my resurrection and ascension to heaven till I come (καὶ τὴν ἐμὴν ἀνάστασιν, καὶ ἀνάληψιν ὁμολογεῖτε, ἄχρις οὗ ἂν ἔλθω.)" the Coptic text of the Coptic liturgies uses, "remember Me," instead of, "and ascension." As such, the text becomes "And confess my resurrection, and remember me till I come."

---

[394] 1 Corinthians 11.26

Bibliography

Primary Sources:

Allen, G. C., trans. *The Didache: The Teachings of the Twelve Apostles*. London: The Astolat Press, 1903.

H G Bishop Serapion, and H G Bishop Youssef. *The Divine Liturgies: The Anaphoras of Saints Basil, Gregory, and Cyril*. 2nd Edition. Dallas: Coptic Orthodox Diocese of the Southern United States, 2007.

Ibn al-Muqaffa', Sāwīris. *The History of the Egyptian Patriarchs known as the Stories of the Holy Churches (Tārikh Paṭārekat al-Kanisah al-Maṣrayah al-Ma'aroūf be-Seyar al-Be'yaah al-Moqadasah)*. Vol. 2.

Ibn Kabar, Shams al-Ri'āsa Abū al-Barakāt, *The Lamp of Darkness and the Clarification of the Service (Miṣbāḥ al-ẓulma wa 'īdāḥ al-khidma)*. Vol 1. Verified by Samir Khalil the Jesuit. Library of al-Karouz, 1971.

Macomber, W.F., *The Anaphora of Saint Mark according to the Kacmarcik codex*, in OCP., 45 (1979).

Macomber, W.F., *The Greek Text of the Coptic Mass and of the Anaphoras of Basil and Gregory According to the Kacmarcik Codex*, Cited by OCP., 43, (1977).

Pope Gabriāl V. *Ritual Order*. Arabic. Cairo: Franciscan Association for Oriental Studies, 1964.

Presbyter Sam'ān Ibn Kalīl. *Meanings of signing the*

Sign of the Cross (M'aānī Rashm al-Ṣalīb). On Spiritual Life and the Rites of the Coptic Orthodox Church. (c. Twelfth-Century).

Yoḥanna Ibn A'bī Zakaria Ibn Sebā'. *Book of the Precious Jewel in Church Sciences (Ketāb al-Jawhara al-Nafīsa Fī 'Oloum al-Kanīsa)*. Arabic. Cairo: New Cairo Printing House, 1966.

Secondary Sources:

Brightman, F. E. *Liturgies Eastern and Western*. Vol. I. Oxford: Clarendon Press, 1896.

Burmester, O. H. E. *The Egyptian of Coptic Church*. Cairo: Coptic Society of Archeology, 1967.

Burmester, O.H.E. *The Greek Kirugmatat, Versicles and Responses, and Hymns in the Coptic Liturgy*. OCP Vol II, N. 3-4, Roma, 1936.

Butler, Alfred J. *The Ancient Coptic Churches of Egypt*. Oxford: Clarendon Press, 1884.

Dix, Gregory. *The shape of the Liturgy*. London: Dacre Press, 1945.

Ignatius Aphrem II, *The Evident Investigations in the Eastern and Western Liturgies (al-Mabāḥth al-jaleya fī al-līturjiat al-sharqīa wa al-gharbeya)*, vol. 1. Deir Al-Sharfa, 1924.

Merzbacher, L, ed. *The Order of Prayer for Divine Service.* New York: Thalmessinger & Cahn, 1863.

Mingana, Alfonse, ed. *Woodbrooke Studies: Christian Documents in Syriac, Arabic, and Garshuni.* Vol. VI. Cambridge: W. Heffer & sons limited, 1933.

Smith, William, and Samuel Cheetham. *Dictionary of Christian Antiquities.* London: William Clowes and Sons, 1876.

Tarby, Andre. *La preire eucharistique de l'Eglise de Jerusalem,* 1972.

Warren, Frederick Edward. *Liturgy and Ritual of the Ante Nicene Church.* London: S.P.C.K., 1912.

Wordsworth, J. *Bishop Sarapion's Prayer Book.* London: Society for Promoting Christian Knowledge, 1899.

Made in the USA
Middletown, DE
08 April 2023

28230124R00109